The Essential
Work Experience Handbook

O'Neill

Gill & Macmillan Ltd
Goldenbridge
Dublin 8

with associated companies throughout the world
www.gillmacmillan.ie

© Arlene Douglas and Séamus O'Neill 2000
0 7171 2952 7

Print origination in Ireland by Andy Gilsenan, Dublin

The paper used in this book is made from the wood pulp of managed forests. For every tree felled, at least one tree is planted, thereby renewing natural resources.

Contents

Chapter 2: The Learner Report

Chapter 3: The Supervisor's Report

Chapter 4: The Organisational Report

Chapter 5: The Vocational Area Report

Chapter 6: The Review and Evaluation Report

PART 2: WORK PRACTICE

Chapter 7: Work Practice

PART 3: WORK BASED LEARNING (APEAL)

Chapter 8: Work Based Learning (APEAL)

PART 4: SAMPLE PORTFOLIOS OF COURSEWORK

Preface

Work experience is a mandatory component of the National Vocational Certificate Level 2 awarded by the National Council for Vocational Awards (NCVA). This book is aimed at *all* Level 2 NCVA students.

This mandatory module incorporates a choice of three modes of undertaking work experience for NCVA post-leaving-certificate students:
* work placement
* work practice
* work based learning (APEAL).

Work placement involves learners gaining suitable work experience that is linked to their vocational area of study in an enterprise or an organisation.

Work practice takes place where, in general, tutors organise simulated or actual work within the college or centre and where students are closely monitored by them.

Work based learning applies to learners that have worked previously in an area connected to their vocational area of study.

Each of these modes and the required portfolio of coursework will be examined in this book.

Part 1 - Work Placement

Part 1 of this book contains the following chapters:
* Chapter 1 explains to the learner the type of preparation and planning that should take place in advance of a student starting work experience. It shows how to identify the skills the learner has and those skills he/she needs to learn. He/she is encouraged to establish clear learning goals. Information on employer obligations and employee rights is included as well as appropriate procedures and documentation used to apply for work experience. This chapter will help the learner to produce a *Planning and Preparation Report* for his/her portfolio of coursework.
* Chapter 2 details how the learner should attempt to document day-to-day work experiences, personal and work-related challenges met as well as any positive learning resulting from both negative and positive experiences. This chapter will help the learner to produce a *Learner Report*.

- Chapter 3 explains the importance of the *Supervisor's Report* and includes guidelines for work experience supervisors.
- Chapter 4 describes how the learner could document the background of his/her work place and its organisational structure and profile. This chapter will help the learner to compile the *Organisational Report* for his/her portfolio of coursework.
- Chapter 5 deals with the different vocational areas and aims to assist learners in producing a *Vocational Area Report* for their portfolio of coursework by providing relevant information including web site addresses for different vocational areas.
- Chapter 6 encourages learners to re-examine the work experience that they gained, to analyse the skills obtained and/or improved on, and to reflect on whether or not they achieved their learning goals stated in their *Planning and Preparation Report*. This chapter will help them to compile a *Review and Evaluation Report*.

Part 2 - Work Practice

- Chapter 7 gives examples of actual work practices and work simulation that could be used to assess the learner's work abilities. This chapter also includes examples of Evidence of Achievement Forms and Skills Verification Forms for different vocational areas. It also outlines the documents required for a portfolio of coursework.

Part 3 - Work Based Learning

- Chapter 8 explains work based learning and the procedure for the Accreditation of Prior Experience, Achievement and Learning (APEAL). This is the method of assessing learners who have gained previous experience of actual work related to their vocational area and whose work experience can be defined as 'substantial, verifiable and relevant' (NCVA 1998). The chapter also outlines any documentation needed for the learner's portfolio of coursework.

Part 4 - Sample Portfolios

Two sample portfolios are contained at the end of this book. They show how portfolios can reflect the individuality of the learner. They should provide a helpful guide for compiling the required documentation.

Note: The word 'customer' is used throughout the text and is interchangeable with the words 'service user' or 'client' depending on the nature of the vocational area. The word 'learner' used throughout the text is interchangeable with the word 'student'.

Introduction

Work experience has been defined as a 'planned experiential learning activity and is an integral part of an educational process' (NCVA Autumn 1998).

There are a number of questions regarding work experience that learners ask frequently:

- the number of hours/days necessary to fulfil work experience requirements
- the appropriate nature and quality of the work experience
- what a portfolio of coursework is and how it is obtained
- how the work experience is assessed
- how to overcome difficulties in securing work experience
- whether prior work/work experience is given due recognition
- who insures the learner
- what a learner should do if things go wrong while on work experience
- what to do in an emergency
- whether there are any special requirements necessary before commencing work experience in some companies or organisations.

The following aims to deal briefly with these questions.

General Requirements for Work Experience

For NCVA purposes, a learner on a work placement or work practice programme must gain a minimum of 80 hours (10-15 days per year) work experience.

- Learners following the work placement mode must gain 10-15 days of work experience in a suitable organisation or enterprise outside of their college or centre.
- Learners following the work practice mode and having actual or simulated work organised within the college or centre by their college or tutor have the same requirement of 10-15 days work experience.
- Learners following the work based learning mode would have experience of previous work. These students only have to submit the portfolio of coursework linked to this previous work.

The various colleges and NCVA centres organise learner timetables differently to suit their own requirements. Some centres or colleges organise a block-release system, e.g. a three-week placement in a company or organisation. Other centres or colleges favour a one-day-per-week work experience programme throughout the academic year. Some operate both systems for different vocational areas.

Nature and Quality of the Work Experience

The nature of the work experience must be relevant to the learner's vocational area of study and it must be verifiable, e.g. the course tutor must be able to contact the supervisor to check a learner's progress.

It is in the learner's own interest to find useful work experience where appropriate skills are acquired — skills that can be directly applied to the world of work. There is little advantage in securing work experience in a work place where the learner would be exposed to only a very narrow range of skills.

Example

Mary, a Business Studies and Computer Applications student, obtained a work placement in AllFiles Travel Ltd. She had hoped to gain useful work experience, using a range of software products — one recommended on her chosen vocational course was Galileo, a reservations program used in travel agencies. Instead, Mary was given filing duties, and she had very little opportunity to familiarise herself with the many software products being used by the other employees. Mary worked mainly in a backroom and had little interaction with other staff or customers. She was happy to learn the different techniques of filing, photo-copying, punching and collating. Looking back, however, Mary said, 'I should have asked the supervisor to allow me to get more involved in the day-to-day working of the business, so that I could have gained a greater variety of skills that would have made me much more employable'.

Learners should not be afraid to ask for more variety in assigned work tasks and to specify the type of work experience that they would like to be gaining.

It would be to the learner's advantage if employers could be encouraged to complete a work experience pre-employment form before learners take up work experience. The form would help ensure that learners will gain an appropriate range of skills to suit their vocational area. A suggested sample form is given on page xiii.

The Portfolio of Coursework

All NCVA students *must* put together a portfolio of coursework in the form of written reports for the work experience undertaken. The portfolio has to contain

(a)   for the work placement and work practice mode:
    1. Evidence of Planning and Preparation
    2. Learner Report
    3. Work Experience Supervisor's Report
    4. Organisational/Vocational Area Profile
    5. Review of Experience

(b)   for the work based learning mode:
    1. Personal Statement
    2. Job Description
    3. Work Place Reference
    4. Organisational/Vocational Area Profile
    5. Review of Experience.

A suggested structure for the portfolio will be examined in detail later.

However, the portfolio should not be interpreted as just a set of written reports on the learner's work experience. Learners are encouraged to include photographs, audio-cassettes, graphic or video evidence to support their written personal accounts of experiences and learning outcomes.

Assessment of Work Experience

Work experience will be assessed as specified by the NCVA:

Placement and Practice Modes		Work Based Learning Mode	
1. Evidence of Planning and Preparation	20%	1. Personal Statement	10%
2. Learner Report	10%	2. Job Description	20%
3. Supervisor's Report	30%	3. Work Place Reference	20%
4. Organisational/ Vocational Area Profile	20%	4. Organisational/ Vocational Area Profile	20%
5. Review of Experience	20%	5. Review of Experience	30%

Securing Work Experience

Learners are encouraged to find their own work experience. If they are having difficulties in this regard, guidance counsellors or course tutors are generally available to make appropriate recommendations.

Prior Work Experience

Regarding the question whether prior work/work experience is given due recognition, please refer to Chapter 8.

Insurance Cover

In some instances, employers do not insure learners on work experience programmes. In these cases, many colleges, vocational schemes or centres make provision with an insurance company to provide cover. Course providers or tutors as well as learners should make sure that adequate insurance cover is in place prior to a learner taking up work experience.

What to Do When Things Go Wrong

Work experience can sometimes be a source of anxiety and pressure for a learner due to a range of circumstances like too many duties, insufficient instruction, isolation, difficulties dealing with customers caused by a lack of experience, and unwillingness of colleagues to help.

When things like this happen and a learner is very unhappy in a particular work situation, he/she should:

1. first consult his/her class tutor and/or guidance counsellor in the college or centre,
2. then approach the supervisor in the work place and explain the problems that exist, and finally
3. take the initiative and confidently suggest ways in which his/her learning might be improved upon in the work place. For this step, he/she should prepare a written list in advance of speaking to the supervisor/manager.

If a situation arises where a learner observes irregular behaviour or practices in a work place, it is likely that he/she may be confused and unsure about what to do. In this case, the learner should

*   refrain from discussing the matter openly with other students, friends or staff members in his/her work placement
*   adopt a professional approach by bringing the matter, in complete confidence, to the attention of the tutor and/or guidance counsellor in the centre or college where he/she is studying
*   follow the advice given by the tutor in co-operation with the guidance counsellor. If it is deemed necessary the matter will be brought to the attention of the appropriate authorities.

What to Do in an Emergency

It would be useful for learners in advance of starting work experience to pick up the Health and Safety Authority leaflet on *Safety in the Work Place* and to check the Safety, Health and Welfare at Work Acts, 1989-93 on page 27 in this book.

At the start of their work experience, learners should request to be shown where all fire exits are and where first aid equipment is located. They should know who is the health and safety representative within the company or organisation.

Learners should also ask to be briefed on the emergency procedures in the event of an accident, for example what action is to be taken if someone falls on the premises. Usually, one person in an organisation is in charge of filling out an accident report form that details the date, time, location and nature of the accident including any witnesses that were present. This person should have been trained to deal effectively and efficiently with emergencies.

Special Requirements for Some Work Places

Most work places do not have special requirements with regard to necessary skills before commencing work experience. Some work places, however, may require skills like typing, word processing or previous experience of telephone work as a prerequisite to starting work experience. For example, learners gaining work experience in an outdoor education centre may be required to be competent swimmers.

In community/child care work places, learners may have to be vaccinated against Hepatitis B or may be required to produce a Garda Clearance Certificate before starting work experience.

SAMPLE PRE-EMPLOYMENT FORM

WORK EXPERIENCE PRE-EMPLOYMENT FORM

(To Be Completed by Employers Before
Work Experience Programme Commences)

Employer Name: Address: Telephone: Supervisor Name: Position: Department/Section: Telephone Extension:	Learner Name: Address: Telephone: College/Centre: Course Title: Class: Tutor Name:

Job Title:

Range of Duties to Be Performed by Learner on Work Experience:

Range of Skills to Be Acquired by Learner on Work Experience:

Signature of Tutor/Teacher/Course Provider Regarding Suitability of
Duties/Skills Listed Above:

Signed: . . . . Status: . . . . Date: . . . .

Supervisor/Employer Signature: . . . . Date: . . . .

PART 1

Work Placement

Work placement means that the learner gains work experience in an established organisation or enterprise that course providers deem suitable. The learner participates in work that is related to the vocational study area that he/she chooses.

THE PORTFOLIO OF COURSEWORK

The following reports have to be compiled by learners taking part in work placement:

1. Planning and Preparation Report
2. Learner Report
3. Work Experience Supervisor's Report
4. Organisational Report *or* Vocational Area Report
5. Review and Evaluation Report.

CHAPTER 1

The Planning and Preparation Report

This chapter is a step-by-step guide to producing evidence of planning and preparation.

The aim of the Planning and Preparation Report is to document the appropriate planning that must take place in advance of a learner getting work experience. We will now examine the contents of the Planning and Preparation Report under the following headings:

1. Report Introduction
2. Skills Audit
3. Learning Goals
4. Document Preparation
5. Interview Preparation Guidelines
6. Job Finding Skills
7. My Rights as an Employee
8. Employer Obligations and Responsibilities
9. Current Legislation with Regard to Employment.

1. REPORT INTRODUCTION

In the report introduction, you should outline the following:

*   Name
*   Award title and code
*   Course title
*   Course description (a brief summary of the nature of the course)
*   Subjects being studied
*   Proposed career path
*   Desired location of future work
*   Work experience day(s)
*   Proposed times allocated to work experience.

2. SKILLS AUDIT

A skills audit involves identifying which skills you have already learned and where you learned them. Skills can be divided into three categories:

1.   Knowing how to use equipment, e.g. computer and telephone. These skills will be referred to as *practical skills*.
2.   Organisational and leadership skills, e.g. rostering in a youth club, babysitting, part-time work at a swimming pool. These skills will be referred to as *personal skills*.
3.   Being able to deal with people, e.g. with teachers or with the manager of a sports team on which you participate. These skills will be referred to as *interpersonal skills*.

You may have acquired many of these skills at home, in school or through pre-vious work situations. Use the following chart to identify which skills you already possess and evaluate them.

Skills Audit					
Skills	Excellent	Very Good	Good	Fair	Poor

* Course providers, supervisors, tutors or teachers of different vocational areas could also select an appropriate set of skills for inclusion on this sheet.

A skills audit also involves explaining how you hope to improve on these existing skills through work experience.

You can use the following checklists to identify which skills you wish to improve on and where you learned them.

(a) Practical Skills

Practical skills can be broadly defined as 'doing skills', e.g. being able to perform certain physical tasks.

Practical Skills Checklist	
Existing practical skills I hope to improve on from this work experience	Where I originally learned these practical skills
1.	1.
2.	2.
3.	3.
4.	4.
5.	5.
6.	6.
7.	7.
8.	8.
9.	9.

(b) Personal Skills

Personal skills can be broadly defined as 'individual skills', e.g. being able to work on one's own initiative and to meet deadlines, possessing a good dress sense, speaking clearly and being able to work under pressure.

Personal Skills Checklist	
Existing personal skills I hope to improve on from this work experience	Where I originally learned these personal skills
1.	1.
2.	2.
3.	3.
4.	4.
5.	5.
6.	6.
7.	7.
8.	8.
9.	9.

(c) Interpersonal Skills

Interpersonal skills can be broadly defined as 'people skills', e.g. being able to deal effectively and efficiently with people and work as part of a team.

In the work place there are three types of interaction:
(i)   dealing with customers
(ii)   dealing with work colleagues/partners
(iii) dealing with employers/managers.

(i) Dealing with Customers
When dealing with customers, there are two types of professional interaction:
• face-to-face interaction
• telephone interaction.

The following questions will help you identify what kind of face-to-face skills you possess:
• Are you good with people?
• Have you a likeable personality?
• Are you a good listener?
• Are you a respectful person?
• Are you tactful?

- Are you obliging?
- Do you always put the customer first?
- If possible would you offer a customer a cup of tea or coffee while he/she is waiting to see a manager?
- Is it true that you never argue with a customer and that you always apologise for any inconvenience even if you know that the customer was at fault?

The following questions will help you identify what kind of telephone skills you possess:

- How do you answer the phone in a work situation?
- Have you adopted a professional telephone manner? (see role play example)
- Do you use the correct greeting based on the time of the day, state your name, offer your help and, if you have to put the caller on hold, ask if he/she wishes to wait or mind holding and wait for his/her answer?

Role Play Example

Telephonist: Good afternoon, Smyth and Cox Brothers Ltd. My name is Mary. How may I help you?

Caller: I wish to speak to Mr. John Smyth, please.

Telephonist: Certainly, Sir. Can I say who is calling, please?

Caller: Yes, thank you. My name is James Turner.

Telephonist: Thank you, Mr. Turner. Would you mind if I put you on hold for a moment while I see if Mr. Smyth is in his office?

Caller: That's fine, thank you.

Telephonist: All right, just hold for a moment, thank you.

- Do you always check with your superior or colleague to see if he/she is free to take the call?
- Do you always obtain the caller's name before you put the call through to a superior or colleague?
- Do you never fail to quickly and efficiently return to the caller and never leave them 'on hold' for longer than a few seconds?
- Do you never fail to efficiently take the caller's name and telephone number if necessary and ask if he/she wishes for you to note what the call was regarding?
- Do you always get the message immediately to the person that it is intended to go to?

(ii) Dealing with Work Colleagues/Partners
Along with the qualities already outlined in the previous paragraphs, the
following are desirable when dealing with work colleagues:
* to be a good communicator (speaking and listening)
* to possess the ability to work effectively and efficiently as part of a team
* to be supportive of colleagues.

The following questions will help you identify whether you have the necessary
skills:
* Are you even-tempered?
* Do you always make the greatest effort to get on well with work colleagues generally?
* Would you cover for a colleague when it is impossible for him/her to
  work?

(iii) Dealing with Employers/Managers
When dealing with employers or managers, an employee must:
* portray a bright, cheery and positive image
* be trustworthy
* be confident regarding his/her abilities
* work on his/her own initiative
* be adaptable
* be flexible regarding work hours
* be committed
* carry out instructions efficiently
* accept constructive criticism about his/her appearance, punctuality and
  general work conduct
* report back to management effectively and efficiently.

To find out whether you possess the necessary skills, answer the following
questions:
* Are you even-tempered?
* Do you never criticise your employer/superior unless it is constructive
  criticism and is non-confrontational?
* Are you able to accept constructive criticism of your work, appearance,
  personality, and punctuality?
* Will you act on suggestions for personal improvements?

Interpersonal Skills Checklist	
Existing interpersonal skills I hope to improve on from this work experience	Where I originally learned these interpersonal skills
1.	1.
2.	2.
3.	3.
4.	4.
5.	5.
6.	6.
7.	7.
8.	8.
9.	9.

3. LEARNING GOALS

Apart from the skills you already possess but hope to improve on during your work experience, you should also try to learn new skills which are linked to the course you are studying. These are your learning goals and they must be clearly identified. You will find that they fall into the same three categories — practical, personal and interpersonal skills.

(a) Practical Skills

Some examples of practical skills that can be learned in different vocational areas are outlined in the following table:

Computers and Business	Beauty Care	Art and Design
• Produce a letter on a word processor • Set up a working database of clients • Design a company leaflet using DTP software • Calculating wages and VAT • Produce a cashflow analysis on a spreadsheet	• Electrolysis • Reflexology • Aromatherapy • Waxing • Facials • Make-up • Eyebrow shaping and trimming	• Design solutions from a given design brief • Use pre-press and press techniques • Geometrical constructions • Use colour separation techniques

$\longrightarrow$

Floristry	Retail
• Cutting • Dried flower arranging • Make 'hand-tie' bouquets • Advising customers and taking orders • Watering and tidying plants • Button-hole • Greening a wreath	• Advertising • Pricing • Costing • Receiving orders and estimating margins • Cash and stock control

Practical Skills Checklist
New practical skills I hope to learn from this work experience
1.
2.
3.
4.
5.
6.
7.
8.
9.

(b) Personal Skills

Examples of personal skills are:
- meeting deadlines
- successfully completing tasks
- being punctual and attending well in the work place
- being dress conscious and aware of organisation/company image
- maintaining confidentiality
- knowing when not to convey an opinion
- knowing how to articulate one's opinion
- being patient and understanding
- being able to take responsibility.

Personal Skills Checklist
New personal skills I hope to learn from this work experience
1.
2.
3.
4.
5.
6.
7.
8.
9.

(c) Interpersonal Skills

You should list those interpersonal skills which you do not possess already but wish to learn in the following list.

Interpersonal Skills Checklist
New interpersonal skills I hope to learn from this work experience
1.
2.
3.
4.
5.
6.
7.
8.
9.

4. DOCUMENT PREPARATION

In preparation for work experience, you should produce:
* a curriculum vitae
* a letter of application.

(a) Sample Curriculum Vitae

CURRICULUM VITAE
Personal

Name: Ciarán Downey
Address: Derrypatrick, Drumree, Co. Meath
Telephone No.:   046-22222
Date of Birth: (does not have to be included based on the Employment
                       Equality Act, 1998)

Education

Moynalvey Primary School, Co. Meath   19XX - 19XX
St. Patrick's College, Navan, Co. Meath   19XX - 19XX

Qualifications

Junior Certificate	**19XX**	
Subject	**Grade**	**Level**
Irish	XX	(Indicate Higher
English	XX	or Common Levels)
Mathematics	XX	
French	XX	
History	XX	
Geography	XX	
Commerce	XX	
Science	XX	

Leaving Certificate	**20XX**	
Subject	**Grade**	**Level**
Irish	XX	(Indicate Higher, Ordinary
English	XX	or Other Levels or Credits
Mathematics	XX	for Leaving Certificate
French	XX	Applied and Leaving Certificate
History	XX	Vocational Programmes)
Economics	XX	
Chemistry	XX	

Work Experience

Position	Firm	Dates
Checkout Cashier	McDonald's	June 19XX - Sept. 19XX
Tour Guide	Tara Heritage Centre	June 19XX - Sept. 19XX
Software Tester	Cell Technology Ltd.	May 20XX - Sept. 20XX

Hobbies and Interests

Basketball, Gaelic Games, Music, and Fishing

Referees

Academic
Name: Mr Patrick Murtagh
Position: Priomh Oide
Address: St. Patrick's College, Navan, Co. Meath
Telephone No: 046-88888

Character
Name: Mr. Val Canavan
Position: Managing Director
Address: Cell Technology Ltd, Bridge Street, Trim, Co. Meath
Telephone No.:   046-28804

Signed: _____   Date: _____

(b) Sample Letter of Application

Derrypatrick
Drumree
Co. Meath
Telephone: 046-22222

Ms Marie O'Neill
Head of Human Resources
Microsoft Inc.
Sandyford Industrial Estate
Dublin 16

19 February 200X

Dear Ms O'Neill

I wish to apply to Microsoft for work experience in the area of Computer Applications and Administration.

$\rightarrow$

I am a student of Business Studies and Computer Applications in Boyne Valley College, Navan, Co. Meath and am keen to gain experience in the rapidly developing computer industry. My interest in computers has grown over the last number of years and I now have a good knowledge of Microsoft packages and good keyboard skills.

The work experience is non-remunerated and is scheduled to run throughout the academic year on Wednesday of each week. While I live at a distance from your company's headquarters I can arrange to travel with a friend who works in the area and I can assure you of my reliability, enthusiasm and willingness to participate fully in any work place task assigned to me.

Enclosed please find a copy of my Curriculum Vitae giving full details of my education and experience to date. I will be pleased to supply references and further information if required.

Yours faithfully

Ciarán Downey

Encl.

5. INTERVIEW PREPARATION GUIDELINES

You need to prepare well for an interview with a prospective employer. Making a few notes might help you. You could use these notes as evidence in your Planning and Preparation Report.

The preparation can be broken down into the following parts:

(a) Work Place Background Analysis

Find out some information about the company or organisation that you are going to be interviewed by, e.g.:
- What is the manager/owner's name?
- What products are produced or what services are offered?
- How many are employed?
- The number of branches nationally or internationally?

(b) Job Background Analysis

Find out about the requirements of the job and what would basically be expected of you. It is always looked on favourably if you telephone the manager who will be interviewing you in advance to enquire about the job if this information is not otherwise readily available to you.

(c) Curriculum Vitae Audit

After the initial greeting, the employer will most likely scan your CV and ask you questions about it. To prepare for this, identify clearly
* your practical skills and where you learned them
* your personal qualities and skills and where you learned them
* your interpersonal skills and where you learned them
* your USP (Unique Selling Point), i.e. why you think that you are suitable for the job, in fact more suitable than anyone else.

Most importantly, link your practical, personal and interpersonal skills with the job that you are being interviewed for.

In summary, to prepare for the interview you must:
* examine your skills, abilities and past work experience
* find out about the nature of the job for which you are being interviewed
* try to relate your skills, abilities and work experience to the needs of the job.

(d) Speech

Anticipate likely questions by consulting with your family and friends. Summarise your answers to these anticipated questions in the form of a pre-pared speech. A confident delivery that shows evidence of planning is essential.

Planning of your speech is the key to good interview technique. It will mini-mise any nervousness you may experience in advance of the interview.

(e) Appearance/Dress and Body Language

Always remember that first impressions at interviews are lasting. It is impor-tant:
* to dress appropriately for the interview (formal dress)
* to pay attention to tidiness and good personal hygiene
* to be aware of your body language, e.g. fidgeting, crossing legs, slouching
* to be aware of the importance of eye contact with the interviewer.

Tips for Interview Techniques

The following newspaper articles provide good tips for interview techniques.

Interview Tips for Job Hunters

The good news for those returning to Ireland is that skills are in high demand and there are plenty of job opportunities. However, bear in mind that employers have increasingly high standards and want to select the best. To prove that you are the best candidate, keep the following in mind.

CVs should be well-presented, two pages long, with no spelling mistakes and highlight your skills and experience. Don't worry about getting your CV bound, it makes no difference to what is inside.

Check every avenue for details of job opportunities. Ask friends, relatives, former employers, look in the newspapers and on the Internet, visit the High Skills Pool Jobs Fair. Working and Living in Ireland details dozens of companies recruiting in 1999.

If you don't hear back from companies, 'phone them. Say when you will be next in Ireland and ask if you can come for an interview.

The standard of job interviews is high. Be honest in what you say and think of factual answers to questions like 'Tell us about yourself' (start with something recent, not your childhood); 'Describe a situation where you have had to deal with stress' (e.g. dealing with an angry person); 'Have you ever had to follow a set of written instructions?'

(remember if you have completed an aptitude test as part of the interview process, this is an example); 'Have you ever had to work with someone who let down the team?' (remember, it takes all sorts — give an accurate example if you have had this experience but remember to mention that person's good points too).

If you are asked about dealing with changing circumstances, remember that flexibility at work is considered very important by employers in Ireland, so avoid describing something that 'wasn't in my job description'.

Never criticise a former employer at interview.

You may find yourself being asked the same questions by different interviewers in the same company. You still need to answer fully each time and be consistent. The interviewers will be comparing notes afterwards and consider consistency as a positive.

You have invaluable international experience from your time abroad. Think about how this can benefit future employers and explain this to them. You need to show the employer that you are interested in them. Find out what you can about the company in advance — most companies will send you information if you contact them.

Prepare a list of questions to ask at interview, for example:

- Why has the vacancy arisen?
- What are your company's/department's goals for the next quarter/year?
- Do you have any plans to expand into new markets?
- What is your most successful product and why?
- What is your company culture — for example, do you work in teams?
- Is training provided? If you have certain skills that you could pass onto others in the company, will you be given that opportunity?
- Do employees meet socially?
- Does the company have links with the community, e.g. sponsoring charities, providing work placements for the unemployed?

And, finally, remember that you may not be offered every job you apply for. However, keep in touch with companies that you do meet, write a thank-you letter after interviews and even if you are rejected first time, ask for feedback and let them know you're interested in future opportunities. Ireland is very small and you are guaranteed to come across the same people again.

Selling Yourself

GETTING THROUGH THE JOB INTERVIEW

The three key attributes towards landing that job are appearance, application and attention. There may be thousands of vacancies out there but you still have to undergo that dreaded interview.

Academic qualifications are not enough in the days when the ability to sell oneself to a prospective employer is king. Many human resources managers look for the other qualities in a person besides their basic qualifications when interviewing for a position.

Good appearance and communications skills are imperative. Some interviewers may also ask the applicant to undergo a psychometric test. This consists of a series of questions that can be used to analyse a candidate's ability and personality.

It involves a rapid personality questionnaire where the candidate is asked to answer 80 questions by determining how well particular adjectives apply to them.

A personality profile of the applicant is then compiled under the following five headings: extroversion, confidence, structural, toughmindedness and conformity.

A concise curriculum vitae is essential. It shouldn't be more than two A4 pages and it should list your work history, education record, achievements as well as personal details such as leisure and sports interests. But remember, the employer doesn't have the time or inclination to wade through pages and pages of your background.

Research the company you are hoping to work for. Familiarise yourself with as much background as you can and have a few questions ready to ask about the company during your interview.

During the interview be positive, show you are flexible and try to be as relaxed as possible. Rehearse the obvious questions such as 'Why do you want to join us?' and 'Why did you leave your last job?'

Don't be afraid to sell yourself. Companies want people who are not afraid to show that they are dynamic and energetic, says Brendan Devine, recruit-

ment specialist with ETC Consultants. Be confident without being cocky. There used to be a tendency to underestimate personal qualities but that has now changed and companies want people who are enthusiastic and energetic, he says.

Avoid extremes of dress or strong perfume as they could result in instant poor impression. Don't be taken in by a relaxed, easy-going manner.

Don't slouch in the chair or fidget. Be positive even if tricky or aggressive questions are thrown at you.

If asked about your previous job do not criticise your former or current employers as this can indicate a lack of loyalty which will count against you.

Finally, don't wait for the employer to get back to you with an answer. Apply for other jobs in the meantime.

Dress and Impress

FIRST IMPRESSIONS AT INTERVIEWS ARE MOST IMPORTANT

Skilled and unskilled workers are likely to be rubbing shoulders these days in the reception rooms of the country's recruitment agencies.

Factory operatives are now visiting the job placement experts instead of turning up 'on the job' seeking work. And many are now being employed on rollover three-month contracts depending on the job.

Manufacturing companies are sourcing more of their staff from employment agencies as the industry struggles to cope with staff shortages. A factory worker will earn a basic £5 to £6 an hour plus perks in Dublin.

'There is a huge demand for people across the board. There has been a 30 to 40 per cent increase in vacancies in all areas of industry,' said Adrian McGennis, of recruitment specialists, the Marlborough Group. All IT positions are in demand plus engineering technicians, accountants and senior sales professionals.

But he said many companies have now changed their recruitment policies. The days of turning up for a one-on-one interview are over. The candidate is likely to undergo a psychometric test, role play and functional examinations in addition to a 45-minute interview.

'We would advise candidates to prepare well for their interview, find out as much about the company and have a number of questions prepared,' said Mr McGennis.

Lack of preparation is one of the biggest criticisms of people going for interviews. 'Some people can appear too arrogant and others reply to questions with a 'yes' or 'no' instead of expanding on their answer.'

If a candidate is unsure about a dress code for an interview be conservative and wear a suit and tie. It is better to be over-dressed. Be yourself, make eye contact and have positive thoughts.

© Independent Newspapers

6. JOB FINDING SKILLS

In the search for a job and/or work experience, many job finding methods are available. These consist of:

1. direct application to a prospective employer combined with a follow-up phone call
2. application in response to a newspaper advertisement or job finder catalogue advertisement
3. use of recruitment agencies which can be found on web sites on the World Wide Web, in the Golden Pages, in the phone book, in job finder catalogues or on notice boards
4. meeting with the personnel officer or manager of an organisation that you are interested in working for
5. networking (using friends or family connections).

A word of advice: Don't wait until you have finished your course to apply for jobs. It is advisable that you should be actively engaged in searching for jobs while on work experience. Keep an eye to suitable positions that match your prospective qualifications.

(a) Newspaper Advertisements

Newspaper advertisements usually contain the following information:

- Job Description: It consists of the job title, location, duties and any other special features attached to the post being advertised.
- Job Specification: It refers to the special qualities, qualifications and skills that are sought by an organisation. At times these are not specified in the advertisement. Instead candidates are encouraged to phone, check an Internet web site or write to the organisation concerned for these details.

Some advertisements require that a job application form be filled in. A completed sample application form can be found on pages 30–31 at the end of this chapter.

Here are two examples of newspaper advertisements connected with two different vocational areas.

(i)   A Childcare Advertisement

ATHLONE COMMUNITY TASKFORCE

ACT is a community group established in 1992 to implement local economy and social development initiatives for the Athlone Urban Area.
We are now seeking to fill the position of:

CHILDCARE DEVELOPMENT WORKER

The successful candidate will assist with the identification, development and implementation of a Community Childcare Strategy for Athlone. The ideal candidate should have a recognised qualification in a Childcare-related area and have at least 3 years experience in Childcare and Community Activities. He/she will have the capacity to devise and implement an integrated cohesive, comprehensive and multi-sectoral approach to Childcare Development in Athlone. He/she will have the skills to interact effectively and to foster co-operation and consensus with a broad range of individuals and groups which includes excellent skills in networking, facilitation, evaluating, administration and capacity building. The position which is funded under the ADM Equal Opportunities Childcare Programme is on a contract basis. Applicants should send their CV before closing date of 1st September to: (mark envelope CDW)

JIMMY KEANE C.E.O.
Athlone Community Taskforce, Parnell Square, Athlone, Co. Westmeath

---

(ii) A Tourism/Sales/Administration Advertisement

KEYCAMP
Holidays

- ## Customer Sales Manager
- ## Group Administration/Superbreak Supervisor
- ## Superbreak/Group Administration Consultant

As part of the Holidaybreak PLC Group, Keycamp Holidays is Ireland's leading self-drive camping and mobile home tour operator. We take pride in delivering the very highest level of service and due to an expanding product range which includes camping holidays and UK hotel breaks as part of our Superbreak brand, we are seeking to appoint experienced professionals to become part of our highly successful team based in Cork. Ideal candidates should satisfy the following criteria for each position.

Customer Sales Manager

Responsible for a team of up to 12 people and with a minimum of 5 years management experience, you will play a key role in the business and sales strategy, setting team and individual targets. Your role will include conducting competitor surveys and comparisons, the training and recruitment of new staff along with the coaching and monitoring of sales calls to evaluate staff performance and identify training needs.
Educated to degree level you should possess the ability to deliver a professional client focused service at all times. With a confident personality and excellent communication skills, you should enjoy dealing with clients at all levels and possess the ability to be able to work on your own initiative or as part of a team, with flexibility towards daily duties and working hours. Travel Industry/Self-Drive Camping Market experience and knowledge of Customer Relations or Public Relations are highly desired.

Group Administration/Superbreak Supervisor

Responsible for a small team, your duties will include the organisation of administration tasks and workloads within this area, dealing with all Group Administration aspects including accounts, invoicing, suppliers state-ments and ticketing. Your duties will also include responsibility for the Superbreak Reservations brand, ensuring all telephone sales are dealt with in a professional manner, the coaching and assisting of staff diffi-culties and the training of new employees.
You should possess a good standard of education with preferably 3 years supervisory (or equivalent) experi-ence within this area. Above all, you should possess excellent organisational skills and be able to 'think on your feet'. This department provides the backbone of the company and you must take pride in what we do and be extremely flexible in your daily duties and working hours. You should be customer service focused and possess a confident and polite telephone manner with excellent written communication skills. Knowledge of Customer Relations is highly desirable.

Superbreak/Group Administration Consultant

Reporting to the Group Administration/Superbreak Supervisor, your prime role will be within tele-sales dealing with the reservation of hotel bookings via a computerised system. In addition, you will support Group Administration with the assisting of tasks in this area that will involve amendments of holidays bookings, invoicing and accounts, suppliers statements and ticketing.
You should possess a good standard of education with a confident and polite telephone manner. With good communication skills, you should be self-motivated with good organisational skills and the ability to deal with clients and suppliers at all levels. You must be flexible in your approach to daily duties and working hours.
Experience within tele-sales or administration, with some knowledge of the hotel industry is highly desired.
For all positions, ideal candidates should possess excellent keyboard skills with a working knowledge of Word and Excel.
Applications, IN WRITING ONLY, enclosing a full CV with a covering letter stating which position you are inter-ested in and why you wish to work for Keycamp Holidays to:

NO CANVASSING

The Human Resources Manager
Keycamp Holidays
78-80 South Mall, Cork. **Closing Date: 10 September**

(b) Job Search on the Internet

The web sites shown below may prove useful in your job search:
www.jobfinder.ie
www.topjobs.ie
www.infolive.ie
www.softskills.ie
www.commerce.ie
www.exp.ie
www.crc-international.com
www.highskillspool.ie
www.corporateskills.com
www.hrm.ie
www.chadmarc.com
www.overseasjobs.com
www.intel.ie
www.john-harty-associates.ie

Handy search engines that can be used to browse the Internet are:
www.ask.com
www.dogpile.com

7. MY RIGHTS AS AN EMPLOYEE

The main duties of the employee are:
* to be available for work and provide a good service
* to obey orders from superiors/employers
* to exercise his/her work duties with diligence and an acceptable level of efficiency
* to maintain confidentiality regarding company information
* to be willing to compensate the employer for any damage caused or wrongful act committed.

8. EMPLOYER OBLIGATIONS AND RESPONSIBILITIES

The main duties of the employer are:
* to recognise equality issues (equal opportunities related to the work place, e.g. gender, age, sexual orientation, ethnicity, race, marital status, etc.)
* to insure employees appropriately in the work place (Most businesses are covered by full public liability insurance.)
* to adhere to the safety, health and welfare legislation
* to respect employee representation by their trade unions
* to pay employees at an appropriate wage level as agreed by the social partners in national agreements such as Partnership 2000. The social

partners include the Government, the Irish Congress of Trade Unions (ICTU), the Irish Business and Employers' Confederation (IBEC), the Irish Tourist Industry Confederation (ITIC), the Small Firms Association (SFA) and others.

- to inform workers of their rights regarding their terms of employment by providing employees with a written statement of these terms
- to provide workers with appropriate minimum notice before the termination of a contract of employment.

9. CURRENT LEGISLATION WITH REGARD TO EMPLOYMENT

(Web site reference: www.irlgov.ie)

The following twelve legal Acts outline the above employee rights and employer obligations.

(a) Maternity Protection Act, 1994

This Act provides maternity protection for an employee who works for eight or more hours per week for the one employer or is employed under a fixed-term contract for in excess of twenty-six weeks.

- Employees are entitled to take time off work for ante-natal and post-natal care.
- Employees have to take fourteen consecutive weeks maternity leave, four of which have to be taken before the end of the week in which the baby is due and four after that week.
- Notice of at least four weeks before departure must be given to the employer.

(b) Parental Leave Act, 1998

This Act gives effect to two main entitlements:

- For men and women to avail of fourteen weeks of unpaid leave to be taken before the child reaches five years of age or, in the case of an adoptive child, to be taken within two years of the adoption order. The employee must have at least one year's continuous service with the employer before he/she is entitled to take parental leave. 'Broken leave' in this regard, i.e. leave taken at different times, can be taken based on an agreement made between the employer and the employee.
- To provide for limited paid leave, not exceeding three days in any twelve consecutive months or five days in any thirty-six consecutive months, where the employee is entitled to *force majeure* leave to enable him/her to deal with family emergencies that result from the injury or illness of a family member, child, adoptive child, spouse, person living as husband or wife with employee, person to whom the employee is, *in loco parentis*, a brother, a sister, parent or grandparent.

(c) Payment of Wages Act, 1991

This entitles every employee to:

- an agreed mode of payment (cheque, bank draft, postal or money order, credit transfer or any other form of mode specified by the minister) excluding cash
- a written statement of gross wages and deductions which should be given to the employee (PAYE and PRSI deductions as well as any other pension contributions or insurance or trade union contributions, etc.)
- protection against unlawful deductions from wages. Employees have the right to complain to a Rights Commissioner and either party can contest the complaint through the Employment Appeals Tribunal.

(d) The Holiday Employee's Act, 1973

This entitles employees to annual leave and holiday pay as follows:

*   To qualify for three weeks annual leave/holidays, an employee must have worked for an employer for at least 120 hours (110 hours if under eighteen years of age) in a calendar month.
*   If an employee is sick during the annual leave period and can provide a medical certificate to verify the illness, this period of illness will not be counted as part of the annual leave.
*   The pay for annual leave must be at the normal weekly rate and must be given in advance of the leave.
*   Pro-rata entitlements for periods of employment of less than a year apply as follows: The employer must compensate for holidays if an employee ceases employment with annual leave still due. This is paid at the rate of 25% of the employee's normal weekly wage where the employee has at least worked 120 hours (110 hours for those under eighteen years of age).
*   Employees are entitled to be paid for public holidays and some church holidays as set out in the Act.

(e) The Worker Protection (Regular Part-Time Employees) Act, 1991

This Act provides that part-time employees working eight or more hours per week who have been in the continuous service of the employer for not less than thirteen weeks (and who are not covered by the Holiday Employee's Act, 1973) are to get annual leave at the rate of six hours for every hundred hours worked.

(f) The Protection of Young Person's (Employment) Act, 1997

This Act aims to protect young workers under the age of eighteen.

*   Any worker under eighteen years of age must produce a birth certificate.
*   Fourteen- to fifteen-year-olds must produce written permission from a parent or guardian. Children over fourteen years of age are permitted to light non-industrial work during school holidays. The work must not interfere with their formal education or be harmful to their health. Workers in this age group must not be employed for a period of fourteen consecutive hours at night including the night shift from 8 p.m. to 8 a.m. This age group should work no more than four consecutive hours without a rest interval.
*   Fifteen- to sixteen-year-olds are limited to a maximum of eight hours in any day and forty hours in any week.
*   Any workers aged fifteen to eighteen must not be employed for a period of twelve consecutive hours at night including the night shift from 10 p.m. to 6 a.m. (The industrial worker's night shift is 8 p.m. to 8 a.m.)

This age group should work no more than five consecutive hours without a rest interval.

- Sixteen- to eighteen-year-olds must not work longer than a maximum of nine hours in any day or forty-five hours in any week.
- The employment of children under fifteen years of age is generally prohibited.

(g) The Employment Equality Act, 1998

This Act defines discrimination as 'the treatment of one person in a less favourable way than another person is, has been or would be treated'. Discrimination is outlawed on nine distinct grounds: gender, marital status, family status, sexual orientation, religious belief, age, disability, race and membership of the traveller community.

(h) The Minimum Notice and Terms of Employment Acts, 1973–94

These Acts entitle employees to information about their terms of employment in writing and the minimum periods of notice to be given by employers and employees when terminating a contract of employment. This applies to employers and employees that normally work eight hours per week or more as stated in the Worker Protection Act, 1991.

A contract of employment, setting out the terms of employment, must be given to the employee within two months of the employment commencement. It should contain:
- full name of the employer and employee
- address of employer
- place of work
- job title and nature of work
- date of commencement of employment
- details of pay including overtime
- commission bonuses, etc.
- pay intervals
- hours of work
- holiday and sick pay entitlements
- pension schemes
- periods of notice required
- expiry date of contract if applicable.

This contract of employment forms the basis of the relationship between the employer and the employee. A sample contract of employment is given at the end of this chapter on page 32.

(i) The Unfair Dismissal Acts, 1977-93

These Acts protect employees from being unfairly dismissed and give redress to those who have been unfairly dismissed. A number of people and bodies are not covered by the Act, for example the Defence Forces, Garda Síochána, FÁS trainees and some state employees.

Grounds for dismissal are
- employee characteristics: lack of skill, of physical or mental ability, inadequate health or inadequate qualifications
- employee conduct: serious misconduct of a continuous nature (isolated incidents are excluded)
- redundancy with agreed fair procedures
- unlawful employees: under-age employees undetected by the employer in the first instance.

(j) The Redundancy Payment Acts, 1967-91

These Acts oblige an employer to pay compensation to employees who are dismissed due to redundancy. A lump sum payment is made to the redundant worker based on:
- age
- years of continuous service
- gross weekly wage.

Redundancy is calculated at
- one week's pay to a maximum of £300, plus
- half of the week's pay for every year of continuous employment between the ages of sixteen and forty-one, plus
- one week's pay for every year of continuous employment from the age of forty-one onwards.

If the employer cannot pay the redundancy, a social insurance fund is operated by the State that compensates the employee.

(k) The Safety, Health and Welfare at Work Acts, 1989–93

These Acts place responsibility on employers to provide a healthy and safe environment for employees to work in. They oblige employers to
- provide safe systems of work and safe machinery as well as appropriate information and training. The Health and Safety Authority (HSA) provides a system of enforcement of the legislation and supplies information on steps towards prevention of accidents and ill-health.
- provide protective clothing or equipment

- make adequate emergency plans for risks
- prepare a written safety statement, detailing risks, potential hazards and details of evidence of having put appropriate safeguards in place.

(l) The Data Protection Act, 1988

The purpose of this Act is to protect personal information on private people stored on computers in different organisations. The following individuals, firms and other bodies who keep personal information on computer are required to register to prevent this information from being abused in any way:
- public authorities and other public sector bodies
- financial institutions, insurance companies and individuals or firms whose business consists wholly or mainly in direct marketing or direct mailing, providing credit references or collecting debts
- any others who keep personal information on computer relating to racial origin, political opinions, religious or other beliefs, sexual life, criminal convictions or health (other than health information on employees kept in the ordinary course of personnel administration and not used or disclosed for any other purpose)
- those whose business consists wholly or partly in processing personal data on behalf of others.

All those who keep personal information on computer, whether or not they are required to register, must comply with the data protection provisions of the Act.

REFRESHER QUESTIONNAIRE:
PLANNING AND PREPARATION REPORT SELF-ASSESSMENT

You may find the following questions helpful for compiling the Planning and Preparation Report.

1. What day or days have I arranged to do work experience and what are my times of work?
2. What existing skills (practical, personal, interpersonal) do I hope to improve on?
3. What specific types of skills are directly connected with the course that I am studying?
4. What new practical, personal and interpersonal skills do I hope to acquire?
5. In what ways had I prepared for interviews?
6. Having found work experience, what job finding skills have I learned?

7.   What are my basic rights as an employee as defined by current legislation?
8.   What are the basic responsibilities of employers as defined by current legislation with regard to health and safety, insurance, fire safety, accident prevention, and union recognition?

LEARNER CHECKLIST FOR THE PLANNING AND PREPARATION REPORT

Headings	Suggested Layout of Contents	Tick	Teacher Comment
Report Introduction	List your name, award title and code, course title and definition, subjects being studied, proposed career path, desired location of future work, work experience days and times allocated for this work experience.		
Skills Audit	List the *existing* • practical skills • personal skills • interpersonal skills you hope to improve on from this work experience and where you learned them.		
Learning Goals	List the *new* • practical skills • personal skills • interpersonal skills you hope to learn from this work experience.		
Document Preparation	Show evidence of document preparation (CV and letter of application).		
Interview Preparation	Show evidence of interview preparation (interview preparation notes).		

Headings	Suggested Layout of Contents	Tick	Teacher Comment
Job Finding Skills	List the job finding skills that you used to find work experience.		
My Rights as an Employee	Summarise your rights as an employee in the context of work experience.		
Employer Obligations and Responsibilities	Summarise your understanding of employer obligations and responsibilities.		

SAMPLE APPLICATION FORM

Application Form

For Office Use Only	Insert Passport Size Photograph
Date/Time Received: Checked by:	

Personal

Name: *Ciarán Downey*   Contact Number(s) *(046) 22222*

Address: *Derrypatrick, Drumree*
Co. Meath

Date of Birth: *28th June 19XX*

Education

Primary School *Moynalvey N.S.*   From: *19XX*   To: *19XX*

Secondary School *St. Patrick's, Navan*   From: *19XX*   To: *19XX*

Examination History

Examinations	Year Taken	Subjects Studied	Level	Grade
Junior/Intermediate Certificate	19XX			
		Irish	O	C3
		English	O	C1
		Mathematics	O	D2
		French	O	B1
		History	O	C1
		Geography	O	C2
		Commerce	O	B3
		Science	O	C2
Leaving Certificate	19XX			
		Irish	O	C2
		English	O	D1
		Mathematics	O	D3
		French	H	D2
		History	O	C2
		Economics	H	C1
		Chemistry	O	C2

Further Education/Training

I AM CURRENTLY STUDYING A COMPUTER APPLICATIONS AND BUSINESS STUDIES COURSE IN CRUMLIN COLLEGE OF BUSINESS AND TECHNICAL STUDIES, DUBLIN.

Employment History and/or Work Experience

Employer Name	Employer Address	Position Held	From	To
McDONALDS	NAVAN, Co. MEATH	CHECKOUT CASHIER	JUNE 19XX	SEPT 19XX
TARA HERITAGE CENTRE	TARA, Co. MEATH	TOUR GUIDE	JUNE 19XX	SEPT 19XX
CELL TECHNOLOGY LTD	TRIM, Co. MEATH	SOFTWARE TESTER	MAY 20XX	SEPT 20XX

Interests/Hobbies:

I ENJOY PLAYING BASKETBALL AND HURLING. I PLAY PIANO AND SOME CLASSICAL GUITAR. COARSE ANGLING IS ONE OF MY FAVOURITE HOBBIES.

Are you a member of any organisations (voluntary or otherwise)?

I AM A MEMBER OF MOYNALVEY G.A.A. CLUB AND WAS CAPTAIN LAST YEAR OF THE MINOR HURLING TEAM.

Why do you think that you are the best person for this job? (Be specific)

I AM COMMITTED AND TRUSTWORTHY AND I ENJOY VERY MUCH WORKING WITH COMPUTERS AS WELL AS WITH PEOPLE. PREVIOUS COMPUTER RELATED EMPLOYMENT COMBINED WITH MY CURRENT COURSE OF STUDY SHOULD INDICATE THAT I AM IDEALLY SUITED TO THE JOB AS ADVERTISED

Referees

Name: MR. PATRICK MURTAGH
Address: ST. PATRICK'S COLLEGE, NAVAN Co. MEATH.
Contact Number: (046) 88888
Status: PRINCIPAL

Name: MR. VAL CANAVAN
Address: CELL TECHNOLOGY LTD, BRIDGE STREET, TRIM Co. MEATH
Contact Number: (046) 28804
Status: MANAGING DIRECTOR

I declare that all details in this form are true to the best of my knowledge

Signature of Applicant: Ciarán Downey   Date 19/XX/XX

SAMPLE CONTRACT OF EMPLOYMENT

Dear

We have a temporary vacancy in .... and I have pleasure in offering you temporary employment in this post.

A Statement of your Terms and Conditions of Employment is enclosed. I should be grateful if you would signify your acceptance of the offer by signing the attached copy of this letter and returning it to ....

Your employment is temporary, commencing on Monday, 19 June 19XX and terminating on Friday, 28 July 19XX. The Unfair Dismissals Act, 1977-1991, shall not apply to a termination consisting only of the expiry of this term without its being renewed.

Please report for work to .... at 9.00 a.m. on .... You should bring with you your Income Tax Form P45. As you will see from the attached Terms and Conditions, your salary will be paid monthly, one month in arrears. This payment will be made on the second Friday of each month for any employment with us during the previous month — therefore, you may be with us 6/7 weeks before you receive any payment. If this is likely to cause you any difficulty you should approach your Assistant Manager concerning the arrangement of advance payment of some of your salary.

If you are unable to start on that date, please contact me without delay. If you require further information or clarification on any aspect of this correspondence, please get in touch with myself at ext. ....

I would like to take this opportunity to wish you every success and happiness during your period of temporary employment with us.

Yours sincerely,

I accept the temporary position as offered. I acknowledge receipt of a Statement of the General Terms and Conditions of my Employment and Staff Rules. I have read these and I accept them as the terms and conditions of my contract of employment with .... I shall report for duty as requested.

SIGNED: _____   DATE: _____

SAMPLE STATEMENT OF TERMS AND CONDITIONS OF EMPLOYMENT

1.   NATURE OF EMPLOYMENT

You will be employed on a temporary basis.

2.   SECRECY

You are required to treat all information gained as a result of your employment with . . . . as strictly confidential, both during and after your employment with . . . . For this purpose you will be required to sign a Declaration of Secrecy Form.

3.   WORKING HOURS

The normal working week is from Monday to Friday inclusive.

The normal working day may vary, but overtime is calculated on a daily basis in respect of each completed quarter-hour worked in excess of 7.25 hours (exclusive of one hour's lunch-break).

Your normal starting and finishing times will be advised to you by your Manager/Head of Department.

Payment for overtime work will be at such rates as are in force from time to time, and is based on completed quarter hours worked in excess of the normal day.

(Details of eligibility and current overtime rates are available from Managers/Heads of Departments).

4.   SALARY

Your salary will be at the rate of . . . . . per week payable monthly. In addition, overtime is payable at the current agreed rates, at present . . . . per hour.

5.   HOLIDAYS

Provided you have worked at least 120 hours in a calendar month, you will be entitled to holidays at the rate of one and three quarters working days per month worked, this leave to be taken by agreement with your Manager/Head of Department but before six months continuous employment has elapsed.

If you have worked less than 120 hours in a calendar month you will be entitled to 6 hours paid leave for every 100 hours worked and to proportionately less for periods of less than 100 hours worked provided:

* you are normally expected to work at least 8 hours per day.
* you have at least 13 weeks continuous service. These 13 weeks are not included when calculating annual leave entitlements.

Holiday pay and payment in lieu of accrued holidays on termination of employment will be paid at the rate of . . . . per day.

You will be entitled to the same bank/public holidays as permanent officials, details of which are available from your Manager/Head of Department (if you have worked 120 hours in the 5 weeks preceding the holiday or have 13 weeks continuous employment and are normally expected to work more than 8 hours a week).

→

6.   **BENEFITS NOT APPLYING TO THIS EMPLOYMENT**
You will not have entitlement to benefits applicable to permanent employees,
e.g. -   club subscriptions
      -   pension benefits
      -   staff loan facilities, etc.

7.   **SICK LEAVE**
If you are unable to attend work because of illness, your Manager/Head of
Department should be notified as early as possible on the first day.
Where you have cumulative service of one year or more you become entitled
to paid certified sick leave up to a maximum of four weeks in any one year.
However there will be no pay for absence due to sick leave during the first
year of employment. You may be required to seek the Company doctors or a
doctor nominated by the Company at any stage during your employment. You
will be entitled to see any medical report made at the request of the Company
and said report shall not be used by . . . . except for lawful purposes.

8.   **NOTICE OF TERMINATION OF EMPLOYMENT**
The Minimum Notice and Terms of Employment Act 1973 will apply to notice
of termination by . . . . or by you of your employment. The statutory
minimum notice which must be given is one week. . . . . reserves the
right to give payment in lieu of notice.

9.   **MATERNITY**
The Maternity Protection of Employees Act 1981 shall apply to female temporary staff regarding maternity leave and the right to return to work. The
requirements in each of sub sections (1) and (2) of Section 22 of the Act are
mandatory. (Details available from Personnel Manager).

10.   **GRIEVANCE AND DISCIPLINARY PROCEDURES**
A listing of the principal staff rules is attached. Detailed Grievance and
Disciplinary Procedures have been devised to ensure that fair and prompt
arrangements exist for dealing with grievance or disciplinary matters. Grievance
and Disciplinary Procedures will be provided on request.

11.   **ALTERATIONS IN TERMS AND CONDITIONS**
Alterations in your Terms and Conditions of Employment will be advised, normally by general Circular or Memorandum to Branches/Departments, as they
occur from time to time.

12.   **GENERAL**
It is understood that you will perform, to the best of your ability, all duties
assigned to you and will at all times obey all reasonable instructions given to
you.

SAMPLE DECLARATION OF SECRECY FORM

Dear Sir/Madam,

I acknowledge receipt of the letter informing me of my contract with
. . . . and I accept the temporary contract on the terms
outlined in that letter.

In addition I hereby **SOLEMNLY AGREE, UNDERTAKE AND DECLARE**:

(1) I will keep secret and never use, attempt to use, divulge or attempt to
divulge information to anyone or body concerning the affairs of . . . . . . or
any of its customers as may come to my knowledge or with which I may
become acquainted while in the employment of . . . . . . or in any other
manner whatsoever, save to other officials of . . . . . . whose province it is to
know the same, or with the consent of . . . . . . or by the authority of a court
of law and I will not by word or deed say or do anything which may prejudice or injure . . . . . . or be calculated to disclose the business or concerns
thereof or of any customer of . . . . These restrictions shall apply
during my employment with . . . . and at any time thereafter.

(2) I will make known without delay to my General Manager and the
Directors of . . . . . . any fraud or irregularities on the part of any employee
or customer of . . . . . . or any other person tending to prejudice . . . . . .
which may come to my knowledge.

(3) During my period of employment with . . . . . . I will not work for a
competitor of . . . . . . and any other work I am/become involved in will not
interfere in any way with my capacity to carry out the duties the bank
require of me.

(4) I will observe all rules and regulations of . . . . . .

SIGNED: _____   **DATE:** _____

WITNESS: _____

CHAPTER 2

The Learner Report

The aim of this report is to test your ability to document a detailed description of the work that was actually undertaken by you while on work experience. Day-to-day experiences, both positive and negative, should be outlined. New learning outcomes and evidence of the ability to learn from negative as well as positive experiences and challenges should be shown.

The Learner Report should be based on the work experience diary located on pages 100-114 at the end of the book. You should fill in one page of your diary for every day of your work experience.

We will now examine the contents of the Learner Report under the following headings:
1.   Report Introduction
2.   Work Description and Skills Gained (Diary Summary)
3.   Challenges Encountered
4.   Positive Learning from Challenges.

1. REPORT INTRODUCTION

In the report introduction, you should outline the following:
*   Name
*   Award title and code
*   Course title
*   Job title, e.g. trainee hairdresser, trainee programmer, trainee travel agent
*   Place of work
*   Branch in country/world (if applicable)
*   Section (if applicable), e.g. hotel restaurant, office or bar
*   Department (if applicable), e.g. sales or accounts department
*   Times of work
*   Name and title of superior(s).

2. WORK DESCRIPTION AND SKILLS GAINED (DIARY SUMMARY)

Your work experience diary will help you to describe the variety of work undertaken and the skills learned or improved upon. It should give a detailed explanation of:

* the variety of work tasks carried out while on work experience from starting to finishing time
* how work was handled
* existing skills improved upon
* new practical, personal or interpersonal skills learned
* personal challenges encountered
* work-related challenges encountered.

(a) Variety of Work Tasks

Some examples of work tasks in different vocational areas are outlined in the following table.

Catering	Fashion Design	Multimedia Production	Childcare
• Food costing • Vegetable preparation • Soup making • Baking • Stirfry techniques	• Embroidery • Printed textiles • Advertising • Fashion buying • Graphic skills	• Digital movie processing • Authoring • Web design • Image processing • Animation	• Games supervision • Montessori supervision • Food preparation • Feeding babies • Changing babies

(b) Skills Gained

In order to identify the skills you gained during work experience, you should reflect on the day-to-day experiences from starting to finishing time and the tasks you undertook. Then you need to categorise your experiences as practical, personal or interpersonal skills you either improved upon or learned.

Here are some examples aimed at explaining how the tasks you are given are categorised as practical, personal or interpersonal skills.

A Computer Student Example

Mary Ryan is a Computer student and has gained work experience in Compumarket Ltd. Her supervisor requested of her, as part of an advertising campaign, to directly mail a variety of catalogues to potential customers. In completing this task the experience would have taught her the following skills:

1. Practical skills
    (a) She learned how to sift through customer records from a database file in order to shortlist appropriate prospective customers.
    (b) She gained experience using the mail merge facility in a word processing program.
2. Personal skills
    (a) She learned how to work on her own initiative.
    (b) She learned how to be more adaptable and flexible.
3. Interpersonal skills
    (a) She learned how to carry out supervisor instructions efficiently.
    (b) She learned how to work efficiently with colleagues to complete the task.

A Tourism Student Example

Colm Downey, a Tourism student on work experience at Going Places Travel Agency, must deal with a client from the enquiry to the booking stage. In completing this task the experience would have taught Colm the following skills:

1. Practical skills
    (a) How to use the computerised Galileo system efficiently. Colm was able to obtain booking information and to book a holiday confidently for the client.
    (b) He learned administration skills which consist of writing a receipt after the client pays by cheque (credit card, cash) and forwarding the receipt to the client.
2. Personal and interpersonal skills
    (a) To be more punctual and improve on attendance
    (b) To be more competent in dealing with awkward customers.

A Hairdressing Student Example

Siobhán McMahon, a Hairdressing student, on work experience at the Wedge Styles salon, learned the following skills:

1. Practical skills
    (a) To wash, set and blow-dry
    (b) To apply a semi-permanent colour and a conditioning treatment.
2. Personal and interpersonal skills
    (a) To acquire a high level of tolerance working in a busy working environment
    (b) To work effectively as part of a multi-skilled team.

A Childcare Student Example

Eileen Daly, a Childcare student, on work experience at Little Treasures crèche, learned the following skills:

1. Practical skills
    (a) To quickly and efficiently change babies' nappies, paying attention to hygiene
    (b) To assist in toilet training toddlers in co-operation with parents
    (c) To assist in introductory Montessori instruction, learning about:
        *   sensorial equipment: educational toys appealing to children's senses
        *   practical life activities: beading, threading, cleaning
        *   mathematical equipment, jig-saws, etc.
        *   language materials: pictures, word matching, sound boxes, etc.
2. Personal skills
    (a) To co-ordinate a range of children's activities, maintaining a good degree of control
    (b) To strictly adhere to the time routine of the crèche for different activities, e.g. meal times, nappy changing and break times, etc.
3. Interpersonal skills
    To delicately and efficiently give comprehensive information to parents regarding their child's or children's progress, using the report book for parents.

An Art and Design Student Example

Séamus Brophy, an Art and Design student, on work experience at Graphic Design Studios, learned the following skills:

1. Practical skills
   (a) To produce a book cover from designs, using QuarkXpress
   (b) To layer photographs, using Adobe Photoshop.
2. Personal and interpersonal skills
   (a) To work on his own initiative
   (b) To contribute his own design ideas to a group discussion.

---

3. CHALLENGES ENCOUNTERED

There are two different types of challenges that a learner may encounter while on work experience:

(a) Personal challenges, e.g.
   - getting to work - good attendance
   - getting to work on time - punctuality
   - completing work tasks – ability to do the work
   - completing working tasks on time – meeting deadlines.

(b) Work-related challenges, e.g.
   - dealing with awkward customers
   - dealing with uncooperative colleagues
   - dealing with a difficult employer/superior.

4. POSITIVE LEARNING FROM CHALLENGES

Under this heading you should describe the positive things you learned both from negative and positive experiences during your work experience. To help you to identify them, you can use the following questions as a self-assessment guide.

(a) Personal Challenges

- Have you become more punctual and has your attendance improved?
- Are you being more accurate and precise in the execution of work tasks?
- Do you get tasks completed on time?
- Do you organise your work tasks in a diary in order of priority?
- Do you attend to work tasks immediately or do you postpone them?

(b) Work-Related Challenges

(i)   Awkward Customers
- Did you learn to listen and take note of the problem?
- Did you apologise for any inconvenience (even though you were not at fault) and maintain a high degree of professional courtesy?
- Did you investigate options to remedy the problem?
- Did you offer to compensate the customer?
- Was the problem resolved in a manner satisfactory to the customer?

(ii)   Difficult Colleagues
- Have you learned to avoid open confrontation with colleagues?
- Do you realise the importance of not backbiting colleagues?
- Did you maintain courtesy towards colleagues at all times?
- Did you articulate your viewpoints to colleagues in a coherent and fair manner?
- Do you realise the importance of looking at the wider picture when it comes to a breakdown of relations between colleagues?

(iii) Difficult Employer/Superior
- Did you learn to accept constructive criticism with dignity?
- Did you articulate your viewpoints to your employer/superior in a calm and coherent manner?
- Have you learned how to work well with a difficult employer/ superior?

REFRESHER QUESTIONNAIRE:
LEARNER REPORT SELF-ASSESSMENT

You may find the following questions helpful for compiling the Learner Report.

1. What day or days did I gain work experience and what were my times of work?
2. What were my day-to-day work experiences from starting to finishing time?
3. What type of work did I undertake? Give a detailed description, indicating new skills learned and/or existing skills that you improved on. Include practical, personal and interpersonal skills and categorise them accordingly.
4. What personal challenges did I encounter, e.g. having difficulty getting to work on time?
5. What work-related challenges did I encounter, e.g. a difficult customer, work colleague or supervisor?

6.   What were the positive things that I learned from the challenges, e.g. have
     I become more tolerant, more able to accept criticism, more adaptable and
     flexible?

LEARNER CHECKLIST FOR THE LEARNER REPORT

Headings	Suggested Layout of Contents	Tick	Teacher Comment
Report Introduction	List your name, award title and code, course title, job title, place of work, branch, section and department (if applicable), times of work, and name and title of superior(s).		
Work Description and Skills Gained	Describe in detail work under-taken by you while on work experience. List the skills you learned or improved on under the headings: • Practical Skills • Personal Skills • Interpersonal Skills.		
Challenges Encountered	List • the personal challenges • the work-related challenges you encountered during work experience.		
Positive Learning from Challenges	List the positive things that you learned from both negative and positive experiences.		
Conclusion	Highlight new learning that has taken place.		

CHAPTER 3

The Supervisor's Report

The Supervisor's Report forms an important part of the overall assessment of work experience. It is a record of observations and comments that the work place supervisor provides on the learner's completion of work experience. For this purpose the supervisor or manager should closely monitor the progress of the work experience participant in the work place.

Note:
1. In the work practice mode where the teacher/tutor/co-ordinator elects to monitor and assess the learner, the teacher/tutor him/herself completes the report. (Work practice will be discussed in Chapter 7.)
2. This report does not apply to APEAL learners as they will already have attained accreditation for current or prior experience of work in a vocational area directly related to the qualification being sought.

GUIDELINES FOR THE SUPERVISOR

It is important that the supervisor completes the form supplied by the NCVA accurately so as to give a measured indication of the learner's abilities.

Supervisors are encouraged to comment on what they may believe are more suitable arrangements for work experience to be conducted, based on the particular vocational area to which their organisation is connected.

They should also maintain regular contact with course providers so as to ensure best quality learner work for the good of both the organisation and the learner. This interaction will lead to enhanced learner performance in the work place. It is also a positive way of addressing any skill shortages that may be apparent.

SAMPLE SUPERVISOR'S REPORT

Supervisor's report
Work Experience (W20008)

Participant's Name _____   Centre/School Name _____   Tel No _____

Organisation/Company Name _____   Supervisor's Name _____   No of days worked _____

Guidelines   This report forms an important part of the overall assessment of work experience for certification at NCVA Level 2.
It should be completed by a supervisor/manager who has observed the participant in the workplace.
Please indicate the participant's performance by placing a tick for each of the criteria under one of the headings.   *Excellent should only be used in cases of outstanding performance.*

Criteria	Excellent	Very Good	Good	Satisfactory	Unsatisfactory	Unable to assess	Further Comments
Interest in the work							Brief description of work undertaken by candidate
Awareness of health & safety practices							
Appropriate dress							
Ability to follow instructions							
Quality of agreed/assigned work							
Practical Skills							Any comments or suggestions on work experience arrangements
Use of workplace equipment							
Punctuality							
Attendance at workplace							
Relating to co-workers							
Relating to supervisor							Any other comments.
Communicating with customers							
Acceptance of direction/criticism							
Initiative							
Adaptability							

Signature of Workplace supervisor _____   Date _____

Issued by National Council for Vocational Awards

(NCVA 1998)

CHAPTER 4

The Organisational Report

The learner has a choice of either compiling a report on the organisation with which he/she has gained work experience (refer to this chapter) or a report on his/her chosen vocational area of study (Chapter 5).

Note: Learners that have current or prior experience of work and are assessed by the work based learning mode (APEAL) are also required to compile either an Organisational or a Vocational Area Report.

The Organisational Report requires the learner to familiarise him/herself with the organisation where he/she has gained work experience. We will now examine the contents of the Organisational Report under the following headings:

1. Report Introduction
2. Background of Organisation
3. Organisational Chart and Functions of Staff
4. Job Specification
5. Internal and External Influences on the Organisation
6. Employment Opportunities in the Organisation
7. Conclusion

1. REPORT INTRODUCTION

In the report introduction, you should outline the following:

- Name
- Award title and code
- Course title
- Job title, e.g. trainee hairdresser, trainee programmer, trainee travel agent
- Place of work
- Branch in country/world (if applicable)
- Section (if applicable), e.g. hotel restaurant, office or bar
- Department (if applicable), e.g. sales or accounts department
- Times of work
- Name and title of superior(s).

2. BACKGROUND OF ORGANISATION

This section of the report should describe:
- the nature of the business (service or product)
- its history and date of establishment
- if it relocated
- the number of branches/sections/departments
- its ownership structure (sole trader, partnership, private or public limited company, state or semi-state body)
- the number of employees (include male/female breakdown)
- the size of the premises.

Visual display charts, like bar and pie charts, can be used to depict data. The following pie chart represents the age and gender breakdown of a company's work force.

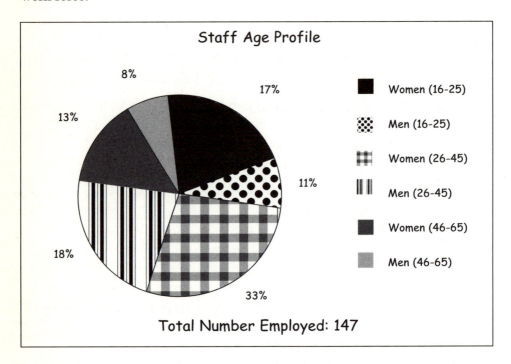

3. ORGANISATIONAL CHART AND FUNCTIONS OF STAFF

You should draw a chart depicting the staff structure and clearly indicating lines of authority. The duties and responsibilities of each staff member mentioned in the chart should be described.

The following are examples of organisational charts from different vocational areas.

(a) Childcare Example

Organisational Chart of The Grove Crèche, Celbridge, Co. Kildare

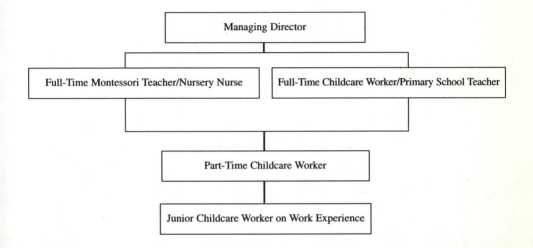

(b) Retail Example

Organisational Chart of SuperStores, Nenagh

Manager

Senior Assistant Manager

Junior Assistant Manager

Junior Assistant Manager

Store Room Supervisor → Store Staff (x 2)

Off Licence Supervisor → Sales Staff (x 2)

Provisions Supervisors (x 2) → Sales Staff (x 2)

Bakery Supervisor → Bakers (x 7)

Butcher Supervisor → Butchers (x 6)

Checkout Supervisors (x 3) → Checkout Attendants (x 25), Bag Packers/Trolley Attendants (x 10)

Fruit and Vegetables Supervisor → Assistants (x 10)

Deli/Pizza Salads Supervisor → Sales Staff (x 4)

(c) Wholesale Example

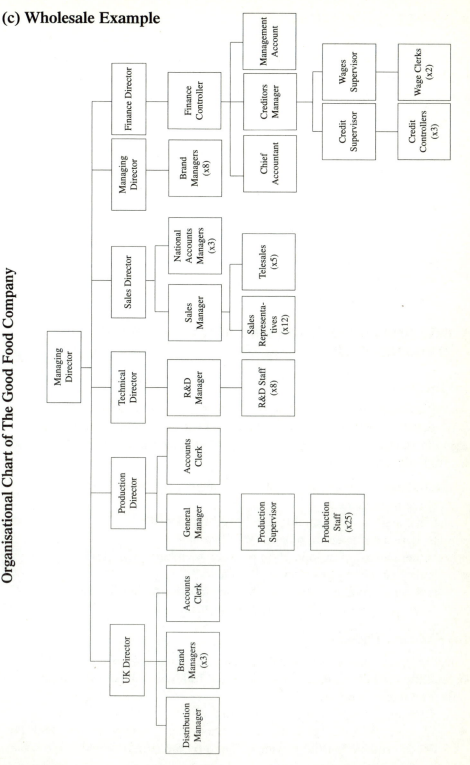

Organisational Chart of The Good Food Company

4. JOB SPECIFICATION

You should select one position in your work experience placement and interview the person who holds the job. You could compile a questionnaire in order
to analyse this job area. Questions regarding qualifications and experience necessary to gain such a job should be included.

Sample Questionnaire:
*   What is your formal job title?
*   What are your duties and areas of responsibility?
*   What qualifications do you think would be necessary to gain a similar
    position to yours?
*   Would it be useful to study other courses and which ones would you rec-
    ommend?
*   How many years' experience do you think would be necessary to gain a
    similar position to yours?
*   Would it be useful to gain a variety of related work experiences and what
    types would you recommend?

5. INTERNAL AND EXTERNAL INFLUENCES ON THE ORGANISATION

(a) Internal Factors

An organisation may be affected by a variety of internal factors that in many
ways dictate how it is being run. You should explore the internal factors that
apply to your work placement and be able to explain how these factors affect
the organisation.

You could use the following questions to identify and reflect on these factors:
*   Is the management style effective?
*   Is the staff suitably qualified and well-motivated?
*   Is there a sufficient number of staff available?
*   Is there an air of co-operation between members of staff?
*   Is there a feeling of belonging to a team?
*   Is there a problem with on-going demands for higher wages?
*   Is the equipment modern and well-serviced?

(b) External Factors

There is also a variety of external factors that in many ways determine how an
organisation is being run. You could use the following questions to identify and
reflect on these factors:
*   Who are the organisation's competitors?
*   What kinds of market forces affect the demand, supply and prices of the
    goods produced or the services offered by the organisation?

- Are deliveries of supplies (incoming raw materials) or products (outgoing deliveries) often late? How are sales affected?
- Have interest rate fluctuations affected the organisation in the past?
- Do currency fluctuations (exporters, importers, tourism, etc.) affect the organisation in any way? How will the change to the euro and European Monetary Union (EMU) affect it?
- How do rising global industrial or occupational wage demands affect the organisation?

In the case of service type organisations the following external factors might be identified:
- Changing birth and death rates (demographics) in a region, affecting, for example, the demand for nursing homes or for childcare facilities
- More mothers deciding to work at home (or telework), leading to a decreased demand for childcare facilities
- Natural disasters, e.g. earthquakes, floods, volcanoes, etc., affecting travel agents and tour operator services
- The growth in e-commerce (buying and selling on the Internet) could adversely affect those organisations not promoting their product or service on the World Wide Web.

Again, you should explore the external factors that apply to your work placement and be able to explain how these factors affect the organisation.

6. EMPLOYMENT OPPORTUNITIES IN THE ORGANISATION

You should examine the different occupations in your work placement and identify areas of opportunity where job prospects might exist or arise, e.g. through retirement, promotions or future expansion.
- Does the business plan to extend its premises in the near future?
- Does the business intend to recruit more staff?
- Does the business plan to expand its range of products or services?
- Does the business plan to relocate?
- Would it be in your interest to study a particular course with a view to gaining a job with the organisation?

7. CONCLUSION

You should summarise in no more than five lines what you have documented in the body of the report.

REFRESHER QUESTIONNAIRE: ORGANISATIONAL REPORT SELF-ASSESSMENT

1. Did I outline the background characteristics of the organisation?
2. Did I describe the nature of the service delivered or products produced?
3. Did I produce an organisational chart and a business profile explaining the range of occupations and functions of the staff members?
4. Did I select one occupational area that interests me and investigate the qualifications and experience required to gain a position like it?
5. Did I identify the internal and external influences affecting the organisation?
6. Did I discuss the employment opportunities that might exist in the organisation?

LEARNER CHECKLIST FOR THE ORGANISATIONAL REPORT

Headings	Suggested Layout of Contents	Tick	Teacher Comment
Report Introduction	List your name, award title and code, course title, job title, place of work, branch, section or department (if applicable), times of work, and name and title of superior(s).		
Background of Organisation	Describe • the service offered or product produced • its history • its location • its branches, departments or sections (if applicable) • its ownership • the number of employees • the size of its premises.		
Organisational Chart and Functions of Staff	• Draw a chart with clear headings and lines of authority indicated. • Describe the duties of staff outlined in your organisational chart.		

Headings	Suggested Layout of Contents	Tick	Teacher Comment
Job Specification	Analyse one job area, outlining the qualifications, variety and duration of experience needed.		
Internal and External Influences on the Organisation	List • the internal factors and • the external factors that affect the organisation.		
Employment Opportunities within the Organisation	Identify possible job opportunities that you think might exist or are likely to arise within the organisation.		
Conclusion	Summarise the main points of the Organisational Report.		

CHAPTER 5

The Vocational Area Report

The learner has a choice of either compiling a report on the organisation with which he/she has gained work experience (refer to Chapter 4) or a report on his/her chosen vocational area of study (refer to this chapter).

The National Vocational Certificate Level 2 is available in over forty different award areas spanning the following: Art and Design, Business Studies and Marketing, Applied Science and Technology, Community Services, Catering, Sport and Recreation, Tourism, Cultural and Heritage Studies, Media and Performing Arts.

The learner opting to compile a Vocational Area Report is required to document information about his/her vocational area of study. He/she could use the following structure for his/her report.

1. REPORT INTRODUCTION

In the report introduction, you should outline the following:
* Name
* Award title and code
* Course title.

2. NATURE OF THE VOCATIONAL AREA

To describe the nature of your vocational area, you could write about:
* its history, nationally or internationally, or any other area or trend in your vocational area of study. A Business and Marketing student, for example, could document the history of banking in Ireland if he/she gained work experience in a financial institution or, if he/she was working in a car sales company, he/she could write about the current trends in the motor car industry.
* the qualifications, years of experience necessary and range of occupations connected with it
* the internal and external factors affecting it
* employment opportunities within your vocational area

- any recent developments connected with it, e.g. government initiatives or new technologies
- any state, semi-state or corporate bodies, friendly societies and charities/caring groups connected with it.

EXTRACT FROM A LEARNER'S VOCATIONAL AREA REPORT

We will now look at a sample of vocational area information.

The following is an extract from a floristry learner's Vocational Area Report where she displays her knowledge regarding the floristry business in Ireland.

Floristry Business in Ireland

Florists working from retail outlets form the core of the flower business. Some people operate a floral design business from home but they are in the minority.

Supplies

Florists can obtain their supplies from several sources:
- The Dublin Flower Market
  The Flower Market's share of the wholesale flower market has declined in recent years. It now has only a 30% share and its business is confined to filling the gaps left by other wholesalers and to sales to florists working from home. The latter are often referred to as 'The Kitchen Sink Brigade' by those in the trade.
- The Dutch 'double-trucks'
  These trucks load up with flowers in Holland, travel over on the ferry and deliver direct to florists all over the country. They cater for almost 65% of the wholesale trade and supply a good variety of flowers. They have the advantage of cutting out the 'middle man', thus their prices are more competitive.
- Van wholesalers like 'Plant Life' or 'Give Joy'
  These companies import directly and then deliver to florists. The main advantage of using this service is that the florist does not have to waste time collecting flowers.
- Purchase direct from Irish growers
  Foliage and flowers can be bought from Irish growers. One bulb farm in North County Dublin supplies directly to florists where they have a regular order.
- Direct import
  For a large business with its own warehousing and cold-room facility it can make sense to import directly from the growers in Holland, Italy, Israel, Isle of Man, etc.

In her report, this learner also provides further information regarding Interflora, teleflorists, the Irish Flower Council and training provisions for florists in Ireland.

USEFUL WEB SITE ADDRESSES AND INFORMATION ON DIFFERENT VOCATIONAL AREAS

General Web Sites

Here are a range of gateway sites to different vocational areas:
*   www.niceone.com
*   www.searchireland.ie
*   www.infosites.net
*   www.scoilnet.ie
*   www.infoseek.com

Sports

*   Sports in Ireland: www.dirl.com
*   Association for Adventure Sports, Long Mile Road, Dublin 12, Tel: (01) 4509845, www.adventuresports.ie
*   Irish Sports Council: www.121.com.au
*   Ireland's Sports Online: www.niceone.com
*   Olympic Council of Ireland, 27 Mespil Road, Dublin 4, Tel: (01) 6680444

Tourism

*   Bord Fáilte: www.ireland.travel.ie
*   Irish Travel Agents Association: www.itaa.ie

Childcare

*   Department of Health and Children, Tel: (01) 6714711, www.doh.ie
*   National Children's Nurseries Association, North Brunswick Street, Dublin 7, Tel: (01) 8722053
*   'Childcare Preschool Services Regulations 1996', £3, from Government Publications Office, Molesworth Street, Dublin 1
*   Pre-School Officer - contact your local Health Board
*   Seven-year tax relief for crèche set-up (if premises being renovated) - information from Revenue Commissioners Office: www.infosite.net, ref: pre-school capital
*   Irish Pre-School Teachers Playgroup Association (IPPA), Two Mile Borris, Thurles, Co. Tipperary, Tel: (0504) 44138
*   Childbirth: www.childbirth.org

Art, Craft and Design

- Irish Artists: www.irishartists.org
- The Concept Design Group: www.conceptdesign.ie
- Sculptor's Society of Ireland: www.iol.ie/~ssi
- Irish Linen Guild: www.irishlinenco.com
- Association of Artists in Ireland, Exchange Hse, Lr Exchange St, Dublin 2, Tel: (01) 6771833

Fashion

- Irish Designers: www.irish-fashion.com
- National College of Art and Design: www.ncad.ie
- Irish Fashion Industry Federation: www.virtco.net

Computers

- National Software Directorate: www.nsd.ie
- Educational Multimedia Corporation: www.educationalmultimedia.com

Business and Secretarial, Administration and Management

- Finfacts (The Irish Business Web Gateway): www.finfacts.ie
- Export (The Essential Resource for Irish Exporters): www.export-ireland.com
- Irish Institute of Secretaries and Administrators, Deloitte & Touche House, Earlsfort Tce, Dublin 2, Tel: (01) 4754433
- Irish Management Institute (IMI), Clonard, Sandyford Road, Dublin 16, Tel: (01) 2956911

Beauty Care

- www.therapies.com/itec/itec.htm

Catering

- CERT: www.cert.ie
- Dublin Institute of Technology: www.dit.ie/tour/index.html

Hairdressing

- FÁS Training: www.fas.ie
- Crumlin College: www.iol.ie/~crumlin

Community Care

- Combat Poverty Agency, 8 Charlemont Street, Dublin 2, Tel: (01) 4783355
- Threshold Ltd, Housing Advice and Research Centre, 19 Mary's Abbey, Dublin 7, Tel: (01) 8726311
- Irish National Organisation of the Unemployed, 8 North Richmond Street, Dublin 1, Tel: (01) 8560088
- Legal Aid Board, St. Stephens Green Hse, Dublin 2, Tel: (01) 6615811

Multimedia and Authoring

- Fusio Ltd: www.fusio.ie
- Scott Computing: www.scott-computing.com
- Image Creation Technology: www.ict.ie

Broadcasting and Film

- Federation of Irish Film Societies Limited, 6 Eustace Street, Dublin 2, Tel: (01) 6794420
- Windmill Lane Studios: www.windmillane.com
- IRTC: www.irtc.ie

SAMPLE INTERNET WEB SITE EXTRACT

Here is a sample web site extract which would be of interest to sports students.

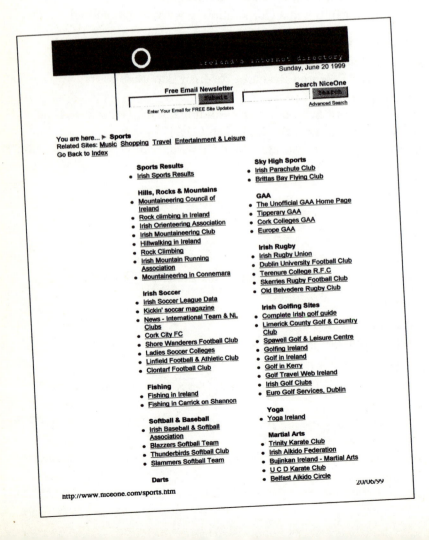

Irish Cycling & Biking
- Irish Cycling
- Mountain Biking
- Mountain Biking Association of Dublin

Sports in Connemara
- Sports in Connemara

Tennis
- Tennis

Racquetball
- Irish Racquetball

Swimming & Water Polo
- UCC Swimming & Water Polo
- Web Swim
- St. Paul's Swimming Club
- UCD Swimming & Waterpolo Club
- Dublin University Swimming & Water Polo Club

Lifesaving & Water Safety
- University of Limerick Lifesaving Club
- Dublin Lifesaving & Lifeguard Club

Rivers & Seas
- Aquaventures
- Maritime Tourism Ltd.

Kayak, Canoe & Rowing
- Irish Rowing
- University of Limerick Kayak Club
- UCD Boat Club Isl&bridge
- Irish Canoe Union
- St Michael's Rowing Club - Limerick
- Liffey Descent
- UCD Canoe Club

Scuba Diving
- Scuba Diving In Ireland
- Scuba Diving
- Dingle Marina Dive Centre Dingle, Kerry

Irish American Football
- Carrickfergus Knights Irish American Football Team

- Irish Dart Association
- International Kenpo Karate Academy

Horse Racing
- The Galway Races
- Irish Horseracing Authority
- The Curragh Racecourse
- Association of Irish Racecourses
- Trinity Racing Society

Sports Clubs
- Network Sports Social Club
- Crusaders Athletic Club
- Rathfarnham Athletic Club

Motor Sports
- Galway Motor Club
- Jordan Grand Prix Ltd
- The Un-official Jordan Grand Prix
- ACJ Timing Homepage
- Brian Duggan's Rally Pages

Sailing
- Irish Dart Assocation
- Glenans Sailing club
- Dublin University Sailing Club, Trinity College, Dublin
- Jo 90's Windsurfing

Anglers
- Ireland's Complete Angling Guide to the Shannon Region
- Headford & Corrib Anglers
- Kinsale Sea angling
- River Ilen Anglers' Club

Rathdrum Rifle & Pistol Club
- Target Rifle News

LEARNER CHECKLIST FOR THE VOCATIONAL AREA REPORT

Headings	Suggested Layout of Contents	Tick	Teacher Comment
Report Introduction	List your name, award title and code, and course title.		
Nature of the Vocational Area	For your chosen vocational area, you could examine: • its history - nationally and/or internationally • the qualifications, years of experience necessary and range of occupations con-nected with it • internal and external factors affecting it • employment opportunities • any recent developments connected with it, e.g. gov-ernment initiatives, new technologies • any state, semi-state or corporate bodies, friendly societies or charities/caring groups connected with it.		
Conclusion	Summarise the main points of your Vocational Area Report.		

CHAPTER 6

The Review and Evaluation Report

The purpose of the Review and Evaluation Report is to critically analyse and evaluate the learner's experience while on work experience. Learners should reflect on whether learning goals were achieved, skills gained or improved upon, and which experiences and challenges were encountered. For this purpose, they should refer to their Planning and Preparation Report, and their Learner Report.

Furthermore, they are encouraged to evaluate how they would now manage a similar work experience situation and what could have been done differently. Finally, learners should outline future plans and what further education and training their qualifications will allow them to avail of.

The following structure could be used for the Review and Evaluation Report:
1. Report Introduction
2. Goals Achieved and Skills Learned
3. Challenges Encountered
4. What Would I Have Done Differently?
5. Future Plans
6. Qualification and Future Training
7. Conclusion.

The learner may find the following questionnaire helpful as a guide to compiling the Review and Evaluation Report.

QUESTIONNAIRE:
REVIEW AND EVALUATION REPORT SELF-ASSESSMENT
1. Referring to the Planning and Preparation Report, and the Learner Report,
   • have my expectations regarding learning goals materialised?
   • have I gained the practical, personal and interpersonal skills I hoped to gain?

2. Referring to the Learner Report,
    *   what positive personal challenges did I learn from?
    *   what negative personal challenges did I learn from?
3. Referring to the Learner Report,
    *   what positive work-related challenges did I learn from?
    *   what negative work-related challenges did I learn from?
4. What would I have done differently if I was starting work experience again?
5. What are my future career plans in the light of my work experience?
6. What work areas will the qualification I expect to gain allow me to work in?
7. What is the nature of the subjects I learned as part of my studies?
8. How are these subjects connected with the work experience I gained?
9. How has the work experience helped me to gain a fuller understanding of the importance of the subjects I am studying as part of my course?
10. What further education and training will my qualifications allow me to avail of?
11. Has this work experience improved me personally, e.g. has it made me more confident, punctual, etc.?
12. Has this work experience improved my work skills, e.g. am I giving greater attention to detail, am I meeting deadlines, etc.?
13. In what ways did this work experience match my expectations?

LEARNER CHECKLIST FOR THE REVIEW AND EVALUATION REPORT

Headings	Suggested Layout of Contents	Tick	Teacher Comment
Report Introduction	List your name, award title and code, course title, job title, place of work, branch/section/ department (if applicable), times of work and name and title of superiors.		
Goals Achieved and Skills Learned	List • which existing skills you improved on • which new skills you learned. (Specify practical, personal and interpersonal skills.) Identify whether or not your learning goals were achieved. Link these points to your Planning and Preparation Report, and your Learner Report.		

Headings	Suggested Layout of Contents	Tick	Teacher Comment
Challenges Encountered	List • which positive and/or negative personal challenges • which positive and/or negative work-related challenges you learned from. Link these to your Learner Report.		
What Would I Have Done Differently?	Describe what you would do differently if you were to start on work experience again.		
Future Plans	Describe your future plans for work, study or otherwise.		
Qualification and Future Training	Describe how this work experience has helped you to focus your career goals. State the qualification that will be awarded to you on the completion of the course you are studying and how relevant it is in relation to your future career path.		
Conclusion	Summarise what you consider were the most useful learning experiences and relate these to the goals you established in the Planning and Preparation Report.		

LEARNER CHECKLIST FOR WORK PLACEMENT

	Tick
Your completed portfolio of coursework should include the following items:	
1. Planning and Preparation Report	☐
2. Learner Report	☐
3. Supervisor's Report (Make sure that your supervisor has fully filled and signed this report.)	☐
4. Organisational or Vocational Area Report	☐
5. Review and Evaluation Report	☐
Include any other written, oral, visual, audio, video or graphical evidence (optional).	

PART 2

Work Practice

Work practice is the involvement of learners in a realistic work programme set up by their course providers or teachers where hands-on experience of the vocational area is gained. Work practice must be carefully planned, structured and monitored. To this end, an appropriate programme of relevant work experiences should be drawn up and implemented by course providers.

Tutors and course providers should be in a position to closely monitor individual learner work. On completing the work practice programme, evidence of achievement should be presented as part of the individual learner's assessment.

THE PORTFOLIO OF COURSEWORK

The following reports have to be compiled by learners taking part in work practice:
*   Planning and Preparation Report
*   Learner Report
*   Work Experience/Work Practice Supervisor's Report
*   Organisational Report *or* Vocational Area Report
*   Review and Evaluation Report.

Refer to Chapters 1-6 for information and checklists concerning the above reports. With reference to the Planning and Preparation Report, some of the self-assessment questions on pp. 27–28 might be redefined for the purpose of work practice as follows:

Question 1: What work tasks have I been allocated for work practice and what is the location and duration of these tasks?

Question 5: How did I prepare in advance of starting simulated work tasks within the college or centre?

Question 6: How would I define good interview techniques and job finding skills?

Learners should also include a CV and work practice preparation notes.

If learners choose to compile an Organisational Report, it will generally consist of a background history and organisational profile of their college or centre.

CHAPTER 7

Work Practice

ORGANISATION OF WORK PRACTICE

To gain relevant work experience, students will usually be allocated work tasks within the college or centre in which they are studying. Here are some examples from different vocational areas:

- Art and Design students could contribute to the design of the college brochure or web site.
- Floristry students could help with the landscaping of the college grounds.
- Receptionist students could deal with queries on the college switch.
- Catering students could plan and help with the canteen menus.
- Marketing students could help in the organisation of the college open day.
- Computer students could create a database of all students in the college.
- Fashion students could help in the organisation of the college fashion show.

Work practice could also take the form of a central event, e.g. a college fashion show. Learners from different vocational areas could take part in the organisation of this event. They could be allocated various tasks, e.g.

- find sponsors
- look for suitable shops that will contribute clothes for the show
- organise the date, venue and layout of venue
- select and train models
- organise public address system, music and choreography
- produce advertising flyers/posters and programme booklets.

EVIDENCE OF ACHIEVEMENT

The teacher or tutor will usually supervise the learner taking part in work practice (however, this can vary) and assess his/her performance.

A major difficulty for many course providers and teachers is how to assess the learner in a work practice situation. To this end, evidence can be gathered and presented in written, oral, visual, or graphical format, depending on the decision of the teacher/tutor. Teachers/tutors are also encouraged to video or audio tape students while they are engaged in work practice tasks to provide evidence of achievement. However, this is optional.

The following are some examples of how students can be assessed, using various methods:

*   Catering students: a combination of video evidence of food preparation by learners and photographs of a variety of their food presentations
*   Art and Floristry students: photographs or video recordings of an art or floristry display
*   Fashion students: video taping a fashion show and the individual learner's management practices in advance and during the show
*   Advertising students: documenting contributions made by advertising learners to a college web site
*   Beauty Therapy students: video of a learner carrying out a manicure procedure or facial and body treatments
*   Hairdressing students: video of a learner performing a perming or colouring procedure
*   Marketing students: video of a learner giving a sales presentation using Microsoft PowerPoint
*   Secretarial students: taping telephone role plays.

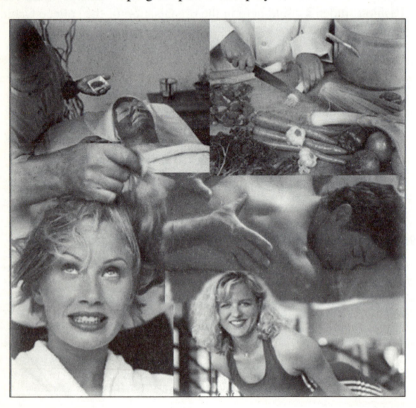

To present evidence in written form, the tutor/supervisor could:
- present a copy of his/her own teacher/supervisor log, verifying the monitoring and assessment of individual learners. This evidence should be dated and signed by the tutor/supervisor.
- present the individual learner assessments in the form of Evidence of Achievement Forms or Skills Verification Forms, samples of which are shown below. These forms can be structured to conform to specific learning outcomes for different vocational areas.

Samples of Evidence of Achievement and Skills Verification Forms

Evidence of Practical Work Experience for Fashion Students
Fashion Show, Coláiste Cluain Mhuire, Ennis, Co. Clare

Student Name: ....

Class: ....

Tutor: ....

Tasks	Fair	Good	Very Good	Excellent	Verified by:	Date

Evidence of Practical Work Experience for Secretarial Students (Skills Verification)

Name: ....

Class: ....

Use of Equipment and Tasks Undertaken	Verified by (Date)	Position of Authority
Using cash register and photocopier		
Using franking machine; sorting and routing post – incoming and outgoing mail, parcel post and couriers; weighing mail; calculating postage		
Maintaining an in/out staff diary and an appointments book		
Filing a range of documents		
Using a fax machine		

Checked and Verified by

_____

Course Supervisor

College Front Office Work Experience for Secretarial/Reception/Tourism Students (Skills Verification)

Name: _____

Class: _____

Experience Gained From _____   To _____

Hours of Experience Gained: _____

Type of Experience Gained: _____

Duties: _____

_____

Challenges Encountered: _____

_____

Verified by: _____

EXAMPLE OF WORK PRACTICE SET UP AND ASSESSMENT

Here is an example of how a work practice task for the telephone reception skills of a secretarial student can be set up and assessed by a combination of methods.

The student acts out a telephone role play with course providers and helpers in a model office environment. The telephone conversation is taped and an Evidence of Achievement Form filled in.

The role play is as follows:

Gillian, the course supervisor, assumes the role of the customer while Stephen, the student, takes the role of the telephonist/receptionist/clerk.

The telephone rings.

Stephen:	Good Morning, Display Systems Ltd. My name is Stephen, how may I help you?
Gillian:	Good Morning. I would like to speak with George Browne, please.
Stephen:	I am sorry but Mr Browne is at a meeting until 11.30 a.m. this morning.

The student and course supervisor continue the conversation. The course provider insists on speaking with Mr Browne. The test for the learner consists of the following:

1.   his ability to handle an awkward caller
2.   his ability to remember to take contact details which include name, telephone number and nature of the enquiry.

Evidence of Achievement Form for 'Telephone Techniques' Test						
Skills	Fair	Good	Very Good	Excellent	Verified By	Date
Ability to handle an awkward caller						
Ability to remember to take contact details						
Interest in customer, politeness and verbal ability						
Accurancy when filling message pad						

LEARNER CHECKLIST FOR WORK PRACTICE

	Tick
Your completed portfolio of coursework should include the following items:	
1. Planning and Preparation Report	☐
2. Learner Report	☐
3. Work Practice Supervisor's Report (Make sure that your tutor/supervisor has fully filled in and signed the report.)	☐
4. Evidence of Achievement (any video, tape, photographs, Evidence of Achievement Forms, teacher/supervisor log or any other evidence available, optional as chosen by teacher/tutor)	☐
5. Organisational Report or Vocational Area Report	☐
6. Review and Evaluation Report	☐

PART 3

Work Based Learning (APEAL)

The work based learning mode is designed to enable learners to gain accreditation for current or prior experience of work in a vocational area directly related to the certificate being sought.

The procedure used to assess prior work based learning is Accreditation of Prior Experience, Achievement and Learning (APEAL). It applies, for example, to those learners who would be re-entering the education system after a number of years. Many are VTOS students (mature students participating in the Vocational Training Opportunity Scheme). Their entitlement to be assessed in this way depends on their employment track record. If a VTOS student, for example, has access to information on his/her previous work place where he/she participated in work that is connected with his/her vocational area of study, he/she need not look for work experience and can gain accreditation through APEAL.

THE PORTFOLIO OF COURSEWORK

The following reports have to be compiled by learners taking part in work based learning:
- Personal Statement
- Job Description
- Work Place Reference
- Organisational Report *or* Vocational Area Report
- Review and Evaluation Report.

CHAPTER 8

Work Based Learning (APEAL)

The contents of the reports for your portfolio of coursework should be as outlined below:

1. PERSONAL STATEMENT

This statement should consist of:
- a detailed account of the reasons why you should be considered for this mode of assessment
- a curriculum vitae.

2. JOB DESCRIPTION

You should outline
- the nature of the position you previously held, e.g. self-employed web site designer or childcare assistant who worked in a crèche
- the duties and responsibilities attached to that position.

3. WORK PLACE REFERENCE

You should submit
- a Supervisor's Report (see Chapter 3) completed by a previous employer
  or
- a reference from a previous employer
  or
- a reference from a customer, client or service user. This would apply to those who were previously self-employed.

4. ORGANISATIONAL OR VOCATIONAL AREA REPORT

You are required to compile either an Organisational Report or a Vocational Area Report. Refer to Chapters 4 and 5 respectively for explanations.

5. REVIEW AND EVALUATION REPORT

You are required to compile a Review and Evaluation Report that retraces previous learning goals, skills gained, challenges encountered, all of which must apply to your previous work experience (refer to Chapter 6).

LEARNER CHECKLIST FOR WORK BASED LEARNING

	Tick
Your completed portfolio of coursework should include the following items:	
1. Report Introduction: List your name, award title and code, course title, and name of previous workplace	☐
2. Personal Statement	☐
3. Job Description	☐
4. Workplace Reference	☐
5. Review and Evaluation Report	☐
Include any other written, oral, visual, audio, video or graphical evidence (optional).	

PART 4

Sample Portfolios of Coursework

The following two portfolios of coursework are examples of how students might put together their portfolios. The style of writing in the two samples differs considerably, thus expressing the unique style of writing of each individual and his/her personality within the work place as well as the scope of individual expression within the framework of the proposed structures.

Computer Student Portfolio (Work Placement)

THE PLANNING AND PREPARATION REPORT

Name: Ronan Geraghty

Course Title: Computer Applications and Business Studies

Course Description: This one-year course at Crumlin College of Further Education offers me the opportunity to gain the essential practical business and computing skills required to gain a job in an Information Technology (IT) related workplace. The course comprises a set of business and complementary computer subjects. On completion of the course, I expect to obtain the NCVA certificate in Information Processing.

Subjects Being Studied: Accounting, Business Law, Business Studies, Database Methods, French, Information Systems, Spreadsheet Methods and Word Processing.

Proposed Career Path: I would like to gain a position in the IT department of a small company while pursuing a diploma in Business Computing by night. This approach would allow me to gain valuable experience in a wide range of IT related disciplines.

Desired Location of Future Work: Eventually, I would like to manage the IT department of a multinational company, hotel or hospital. As a first step in my proposed career path and as a compulsory component of this course, I hope to gain work in the computer department of St. Vincent's Hospital, Ballsbridge, Dublin.

Work Experience Day: Each Friday over the academic year

Proposed Times: 9 a.m. - 5 p.m.

Skills Audit

I will now outline skills and qualities that I possess in relation to those that may be relevant during my proposed work placement.

Personal Skills/Qualities
- Adaptability: I can adapt quickly to new work situations.
- Logical: I adopt a logical approach to problem solving.
- Reliable: I am punctual and can work on my own initiative.
- Persistence: I stick with a task until it is completed.
- Attentiveness: I listen carefully.

Practical Skills
- Software installation: I have installed software on personal computers.
- Software usage: I have gained a reasonable competence in using the most frequently-used computer applications (word processing and spreadsheets) during transition year at school.

Interpersonal Skills
- Able team worker: I have worked as part of a team at McDonald's Restaurant.
- Good communicator: I listen carefully and articulate my point of view well.
- Tolerant: I believe that I am tolerant of the opinions of others.

Learning Goals

My goals, during the work placement, are to gain new skills and improve upon existing ones. I will now examine my goals under the aforementioned skills' headings.

Personal Skills/Qualities
- Self-esteem: I hope to gain confidence in my own abilities.
- Meeting deadlines: I hope to improve upon my completing of all tasks on time.

Practical Skills
- Hardware upgrading: I wish to gain competence in installing disk drives, memory chips and interface cards in a computer.
- Software configuration: After installing software on a computer, I hope to learn how to configure it to suit the needs of the hospital.
- Software usage: I hope to learn how to use new applications software.

Interpersonal Skills
- Positive contribution: I hope to make a positive contribution to meetings with fellow workers.
- Tactfulness: I hope to tread carefully in dealings with fellow workers and not to blurt out the first thing that comes to mind.

Document Preparation

I now include the documentation that passed between Dermot Murtagh, head of the computer department at St. Vincent's Hospital, and myself prior to my taking up the work placement.

1. Letter of Application

---

32 Dargle View
Rathfarnham
Dublin 16

Mr Dermot Murtagh
IT Manager
Computer Department
St. Vincent's Hospital
Ballsbridge
Dublin 4

25 August 2000

Dear Mr Murtagh

I wish to apply for work experience with your department. I have enrolled in a Computer Applications and Business Studies course at Crumlin College, Crumlin Road, Dublin 12 and work experience is a compulsory component of the course. The work placement runs for this full academic year and is scheduled for Friday of each week.

Enclosed please find a copy of my Curriculum Vitae and an outline of my course. I look forward to hearing from you.

Yours faithfully
Ronan Geraghty

---

2. Curriculum Vitae

Personal

Name: Ronan Geraghty

Address: 32 Dargle View, Rathfarnham, Dublin 16

Telephone No.: 01-2963114

Date of Birth: 21 February 1982

→

Education

Scoil Naithi, Ballinteer, Dublin 16	1987 - 1995
Ballinteer Community School	1995 - 2000
Crumlin College of Further Education	2000 - 2001

Qualifications

Junior Certificate 1998

Subject	Grade	Level
Irish	C2	Lower
English	C1	Higher
Mathematics	B3	Higher
French	B1	Common
History	C1	Common
Geography	A2	Common
Commerce	B1	Common
Science	C2	Common

Leaving Certificate 2000

Subject	Grade	Level
Irish	C2	Lower
English	C2	Higher
Mathematics	B1	Lower
French	D1	Higher
History	A2	Higher
Economics	C2	Lower
Chemistry	B3	Lower

Work Experience

Position	Firm	Dates
Checkout Cashier	McDonald's	June 1998 - Sept. 1998
Tour Guide	Rathfarnham Castle	June 1999 - Sept. 1999

Hobbies and Interests

Gaelic Games, Soccer, Music, Dancing and Cinema

Referees
Academic

Name:	Ms Patricia Logan
Position:	Principal
Address:	Ballinteer Community School, Ballinteer, Dublin 16
Telephone No:	01-2923522

→

Character

Name: Mr. Hugh McCann
Position: Branch Manager
Address: McDonald's Restaurant, Nutgrove SC, Dublin 14
Telephone No.:   01-2928117

Signed: _____   *Date:* _____

---

3. Letter of Reply

> Computer Department
> St. Vincent's Hospital
> Ballsbridge
> Dublin 4

32 Dargle View
Rathfarnham
Dublin 16

30 August 2000

Dear Ronan

We would be delighted to facilitate you in your quest for a work placement. Our department, set up in 1972 with four employees, now employs eleven people. We look after the computing needs of the entire hospital.

Ronan, I would like you to call for an appointment to discuss the nature of the work we carry out. We could then decide on the most suitable area in which you could be deployed.

I look forward to hearing from you.

Yours faithfully

Dermot Murtagh
IT Department

Work Schedule

After meeting with Dermot, it was decided that I would be involved in some or all of the following types of work:

- installing software, e.g. anti-virus, new versions of Microsoft products, etc.
- customising Windows
- upgrading hardware, e.g. memory, hard disk upgrades
- installing interface cards
- backing up hospital records
- data entry.

Employment and Legislation

Confidentiality

As part of my work placement, I may be asked to work on data entry. This means that I may have access to information of a confidential nature. I am bound by the hospital authorities not to divulge any information to third parties.

Health and Safety

As you would expect, St. Vincent's Hospital takes great care to ensure that the health and safety of its employees and patients are not endangered in any way. The hospital authorities have implemented an elaborate set of procedures to ensure that the working conditions of its employees fully comply with the Safety, Health and Welfare at Work Acts. This set of procedures ranges from a comprehensive fire plan to a policy on the handling of surgical waste.

THE LEARNER REPORT

Description of the Work Undertaken

My work placement at St. Vincent's Hospital exposed me to a range of working experiences:

1. Upgrading Hardware

Most of the personal computers in the hospital were more than two years old and we had to install:

* more Random Access Memory (RAM)
* bigger hard disks
* network cards - this was to facilitate the provision of a local area network that would allow relevant staff to access patient records from various locations around the hospital.

The bulk of this work was carried out during October and November.

2. Upgrading Software

We had to install the latest version of Microsoft Windows and current anti-virus software on each personal computer. I had to configure the Windows environment to suit the needs of individual members.

We also installed voice-recognition software — *IBM Voice Gold* — on some consultants' computers. This meant that the consultants could compile patient reports easily while greatly reducing the amount of typing required. The bulk of this interesting work was carried out between mid-November and Christmas.

3. Backing up Hospital Records

Much of January and February was spent backing up hospital records. This was a time-consuming and laborious task. I had to copy the contents of each hard disk onto tape, using a tape streamer. I was glad of the occasional problem with Windows on a computer at a nursing station to take me away from the monotony!

4. Data Entry

The range of material which I had to key made an apparently dull job quite interesting. Some of the work involved keying and saving patient records from old computer listings into Microsoft Access database files. The nature of the work gave me a greater understanding of how Microsoft Access works and how it is used in the world of work.

Initially, Dermot dictated all replies to his mail using a dictaphone. I then took the dictaphone tape and typed the replies. However, as the year passed, he allowed me to respond to the less important mail. For example, I had to write a letter to a new company who wanted to sell us some laser printers. As we were fully equipped with new laser printers, we had to decline the unbeatable offer! Data entry took up most of my time at the hospital during March and April.

Reflections on Experiences at the Time

My work experience diary contains accounts of various experiences that I had during my work placement at St. Vincent's Hospital. I will now reflect on some of these experiences.

Nervousness

I was very nervous on my first day. I feared that I would be left on my own to carry out tasks that were beyond my capabilities. I had a premonition that I would damage a computer that was essential to the life of a critically ill patient! My nervousness and fears soon evaporated as I made new friends and got to know how the department functioned.

Tiredness

Initially, I found the working day very demanding. On each work placement day, I left home at 7.30 a.m. and usually did not arrive back again until after 7.15 p.m. I felt mentally and physically exhausted by the end of the day. I would say, without hesitation, that my work placement days at St. Vincent's Hospital were more demanding than any day at college.

The Importance of Our Work

It soon became clear to me how important the contribution of a computer department is to the smooth running of a hospital. For example, when a critically ill former patient was admitted to the hospital, his records could be accessed instantaneously on the hospital's computer system by the consultant on duty. These records contained details of medication previously prescribed as well as the patient's blood group, etc.

Belonging to a Team

I realised quite quickly how the members of the department depended on each other. For example, staff installing software could not proceed until staff installing new hard disks had completed their work first. I got a sense of belonging to a team where each member cared for and depended upon every other member. Each Friday (my work placement day), the staff would usually go for an end-of-week drink after work. This experience allowed me to meet department members in a relaxed social setting.

Sense of Fun

On my second day, a member of the department asked me to go up to David's office and get a box of pacemakers for installation in fourteen old computers. When I carried out the request, David laughed heartily! 'We install pacemakers in patients, not computers' was his reply! The entire department got a lift out of this blooding of the new boy!

Challenges Encountered

Personal

I had to overcome an initial feeling of anxiety during my work placement. I feared that I would be working with a group of technical wizards who would not tolerate a person trying to take his first steps in the world of Information Technology. During my first day, one member of the department quizzed me on various aspects of my course. I felt that he was trying to expose a lack of computer knowledge and I resented this. Some months later, I found out that he was only trying to be friendly and attempting to integrate me into the group's discussion at the lunch break.

Work-Related

I found the working day quite long. I felt under pressure to meet deadlines. For example, the entire department was under a good deal of pressure when trying to complete upgrading the older personal computers before the software installation stage.

Positive Learning

Personal

I made a number of good friends and learned how to contribute to function as part of a team.

Work-Related

During the work placement, I learned a wide range of practical IT skills. I now feel that I am competent in upgrading the hardware of an old personal computer, e.g. installing more memory, new hard disks, etc.

New Learning

I gained a good deal of practical IT skills:

*   Hardware upgrading: I gained competence in the installation of disk drives, memory chips and interface cards.
*   Software configuration: After installing software on a computer, I learned how to configure it to suit the needs of some members of the hospital staff.
*   Software usage: I gained valuable experience in using current applications software in a real work situation, e.g. creating a database using Microsoft Access.

I learned the level of competence required of computer professionals in a real work situation.

THE ORGANISATIONAL REPORT

I gained my work placement in the computer department of St Vincent's Hospital. This department is responsible for:

*   providing technical backup to the administration department
*   ensuring the computer facilities are capable of maintaining up-to-date confidential patient records
*   ensuring the computer facilities are capable of maintaining up-to-date details on drugs and patient care management
*   providing IT backup to the hospital's research programmes
*   ensuring that computers controlling essential hospital equipment, e.g. computers used in the critical care unit, are modern and well maintained.

The department comprises eleven team members:

*   IT Manager
*   Senior Software Developer
*   Software Developers
*   Network Manager
*   Senior Technician
*   Technicians
*   Secretary.

Department Structure

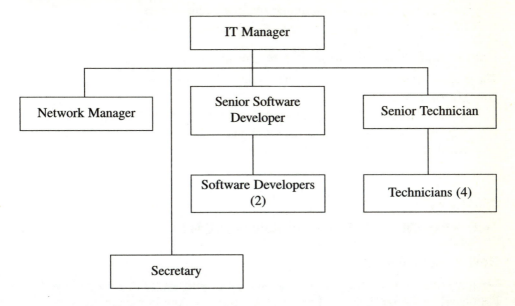

Staff Member's Duties

I will now examine the duties of one member of the department - Marie
Cummins (Network Manager).

Marie is responsible for:
• the day-to-day administration of the hospital's local area network
• managing the Intranet and Internet facilities on the network
• ongoing development of the services provided on the network
• reporting to the IT manager possible future outlay costs.

Marie, after graduating from University College, Dublin, in 1997 with a B.Sc.
Degree (Hons) in Computer Science, joined Networking Essentials, a company
specialising in the installation of Novell and 3Com networks. Marie studied for
the Microsoft Certified Systems Engineers examination (MCSE) by night.
After completing her MCSE in 1999, Marie joined the computer department at
St. Vincent's Hospital.

Internal Factors Affecting the Organisation
• Appointment of a new hospital management team
• Members of the department who may leave
• Changes to the department's budget

External Factors Affecting the Organisation

- Rapid change in information and medical technologies
- Difficulties in recruiting more computer staff

Employment Opportunities in the Department

The employment opportunities in the computer department at St. Vincent's are good. Dermot hopes to recruit:

- a Web Master to develop and maintain the hospital web site
- a training consultant (part-time) to manage all staff training requirements with regard to information technology.

THE REVIEW AND EVALUATION REPORT

Review of Learning Goals

I believe that I have achieved my learning goals with varied degrees of success. I am more self-confident and I should have little anxiety in meeting and working with new people in the future. In working in an environment where deadlines must be kept, I have learned to tackle problems immediately and not allow a backlog of work to build up.

I have gained many new practical computing skills during my time at St. Vincent's Hospital. Among the many skills acquired, I am now competent in:

- installing hard and CD-ROM drives
- performing memory upgrades
- configuring software for new work situations.

My interpersonal skills have also improved. I have no difficulty in making contributions at meetings and I have adopted a more diplomatic approach to problem solving.

Critical Reflection on Personal and Vocational Experience

In summary, I believe that my time at St. Vincent's Hospital has helped me greatly to mature as a person in my own right. The work placement was a very important aspect of my course as it gave me a real insight into the world of work. I now know the joy of contributing to the chats on football or on the latest film during our lunch breaks as well as working under the intense stress of completing a software configuration in time for a consultants' meeting.

Discussion on Personal and Work-Related Learning

My learning during the work placement was very different to that which took place at college. My experiences in the many real work situations contributed as a by-product to my personal and work skills education. My personal development was greatly enriched by interacting with adults of different ages who possess different life experiences.

At college, on the other hand, my learning is guided by a lecturer. Practical skills are imparted and reinforced through practice. My personal development is somewhat limited in that I am interacting with people of my own age who would have quite a narrower range of life experiences than the aforementioned co-workers at St. Vincent's Hospital.

What Would I Do Differently?

The old adage 'It is easy to be wise in hindsight' is applicable to my time on work placement.

As I found the journey in traffic to and from the work placement quite arduous, I would seek a work placement at a hospital nearer to my home.

If I was starting another work placement at St. Vincent's, I would:
• not be as reticent in asking for help
• ask to be involved in the development of the hospital web site
• ask for access to my own personal computer.

Outline of Future Plans

Having worked on a range of IT projects at St. Vincent's Hospital, I would aspire to becoming a computer professional. To this end, I would like to study for a diploma/degree in Information Technology. I would then like to pursue a career in data communications and/or networking.

The Nature of the Qualification

On completing the course, I hope to gain the NCVA Certificate in Information Processing. The certificate would greatly enhance my prospects of obtaining a position in the IT department of an organisation. I am, however, hopeful of gaining a sufficiently high mark in the award in order to secure a place on an IT diploma course at a third level college for the forthcoming academic year.

Floristry and Interior Landscaping Student Portfolio (Work Placement)

THE PLANNING AND PREPARATION REPORT

Name: Síle O'Connor

Course Title: Floristry and Interior Landscaping

Course Description: This is a one-year course offering me the opportunity to gain the NCVA Certificate in Floristry and Landscaping.

Subjects Being Studied: Floristry, Floriculture, Retail Display, Applied Marketing, Retail Selling, Customer Services, Health, Safety and Hygiene, Communications and Small Business Accounts.

Proposed Career Path: To set up my own flower shop business.

Desired Location of Future Work: Near home or at home.

Work Experience Day: Each Saturday (rearranged instead of Friday) over the academic year.

Times: 9a.m. to 4p.m. or 6p.m. (varying).

My Skills Audit

I think that my previous extensive work experience that I gained before I got married some years ago gives me an added advantage when it comes to life skills. I think I have:

- good organisational skills gained from having reared children, looked after a house and having worked in a local shop some years ago
- good team-worker characteristics
- the willingness to take the initiative and accept responsibility
- the ability to do some basic typing and a bit of word processing.

I have a good mixture of desirable attributes. I would like people to realise that I'm an honest, reliable and hard-working individual who is good with people. I hope that the modest mix of personal, interpersonal and practical skills that I have gained so far in life will be an advantage when I start work experience shortly.

My Goals for Work Experience

My aims are
* to get first-hand experience of retail floristry
* to develop my floristry skills and techniques
* to learn how to deal efficiently with customers and how to skillfully determine their needs based on the knowledge that I expect to gain
* to learn how to offer appropriate advice to customers
* to learn how to use a cash register, handle cash, credit cards, laser cards and cheques
* to build up enough confidence to re-enter the workplace
* to learn how a retail flower business is organised
* to make contacts for possible future employment.

Legislation

I realise the importance of having some prior knowledge of my rights as a full-time employee in the workplace and of employer obligations. The following is a summary of what I have learned from the course that I am studying:

The Safety, Health and Welfare at Work Acts, 1989-93 require employers to provide a safe place of work for their employees by identifying risks and taking all possible measures to eliminate them. The main hazards in floristry work that employers have to minimise are:
* cuts from knives and scissors
* slipping on wet floors or leaves
* burns from hot glue guns
* skin irritation from working with wet materials, bleach, and plant material
* electric shock form handling electrical appliances with wet hands
* back injury from lifting buckets of water that are too heavy
* shoulder and neck injury from stretching to reach flowers displayed up high
* risk of theft and violent attack.

The legislation relating to employment includes provisions covering
* the minimum periods of notice to be given by both employee and employer when ending an employment contract
* the right to equal pay for men and women doing the same work
* the protection of direct and indirect discrimination between male and female employees on grounds of sex or marital status
* entitlements to paid holidays and maternity leave.

Evidence of my Search for Work Experience

[*The following documents should be attached to this report to prove that the
student was active in looking for work experience:*

- *letters of application for work experience*
- *letter of invitation to interview (if applicable)*
- *personal account of the student's quest to find work experience with
  names of organisations and reference names and phone numbers of
  supervisors/managers*
- *a curriculum vitae*
- *any other supporting documentation.*]

My Quest to Find Work Experience

Last year I had applied to Marie's Flowers in the People Shopping Centre for a
part-time job but I was unsuccessful. Having been accepted on the Floristry
Course in the college, I decided to look for work experience in the same place.
They were happy to accept me and I was delighted to get the opportunity to
gain the experience that I need.

This experience made me realise that the key to re-entering the workforce is
through gaining appropriate skills, qualifications and work experience.

THE LEARNER REPORT

When I was first invited to meet with the senior manager and shop manager, I
dressed well and had prepared notes on the interview, hoping that it wouldn't
be too intimidating. They seemed impressed with my enthusiastic attitude but
they both agreed that Friday was too busy a day to train me, so it was agreed
that I would work in the shop on Saturday instead. It was left up to the
manager and myself to work out my hours of work. I initially worked from
9 a.m. to 1 p.m., then from 9 a.m. to 4 p.m., and finally from 9 a.m. to 6 p.m.

Summary of my Diary that I Kept during my Work Experience

I completed twenty-one days work experience (more than I needed) between
September and April 1999. In addition I worked six extra days over Christmas,
Valentine's Day and Mother's Day when the shop needed extra help. I was
paid for those days.

My usual Saturday routine was:
- to water and tidy the houseplants
- to keep the shop, especially the floor, tidy and free of debris
- to wrap customers' purchases and use the cash register
- to make ribbon bows for future use.

As I became more familiar with the work I also
- made 'hand-tie' bouquets
- advised customers on suitable bouquet combinations
- took orders for delivery from the shop and through Interflora
- answered the telephone.

In addition I was allowed to watch and learn from the other workers and I was shown how to do various things, e.g. a buttonhole, greening a wreath and making up a basket of flowers.

THE ORGANISATIONAL REPORT

History, Location and Structure of Marie's Flowers

The first unit of this chain of flower shops was opened in the Abbey Shopping Centre in Francis Street, Cork, in 1979. Currently six retail branches exist all around the country.

Organisational Chart of Branches of Marie's Flowers in Ireland

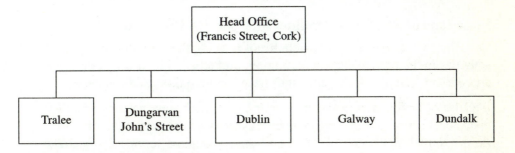

Staffing

The overall number of staff for the whole chain of shops is about 20 – including part-time employees. In the Dungarvan branch where I worked staffing levels varied from two to three during the week to four on a Saturday. At exceptionally busy times, for example on Valentine's Day and on Mother's Day, the staff needed rises to six or seven. That really tests everyone's ability to co-operate and work as part of a successful team, especially when work space is limited!

Organisational Chart of Staff Employed in the Dungarvan Branch of Marie's Flowers

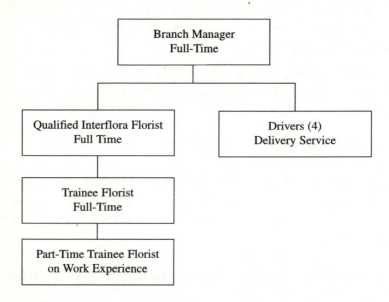

Functions of Staff, and Product and Service Provided

The Branch Manager is responsible for overseeing the smooth running of all activities in the branch and for sorting out problems with customer orders where appropriate. She also looks after staff needs and monitors staff generally.

Because of its location near a main entrance to the shopping centre and its open access structure, the business enjoys an excellent passing trade. The florists, both trainee and fully trained florist, provide a service that includes pre-packaged bunches of assorted flowers, houseplants and planted baskets. Bouquets, small arrangements, wreaths and corsages are made to order by the qualified florist. Ancillary items such as vases, candles and floral sundries are also for sale in the shop.

A delivery service is provided for flower sales to personal customers. Orders are taken for delivery locally by drivers that are employed by the business. Some orders are processed through Interflora for delivery outside of the local catchment area and around the world. The shop accepts credit card telephone orders and wedding work. Outside decorating is done through the head office.

The head office provides after-hours training one night a week and pays the Interflora exam fees for their employees.

THE REVIEW AND EVALUATION REPORT

The work experience aspect of the course that I am studying caused me the most anxiety and apprehension initially. Walking into that shop on the first day wasn't easy! But as time passed I settled in, gained confidence and began to enjoy the work. The people working with me were friendly, helpful, considerate and tolerant. My supervisor was very supportive. I was regularly complimented on work done and any correction was presented as advice rather than criticism. My supervisor was always on hand to provide assistance and rectify any mistakes.

I achieved most of the goals that I set myself. I certainly did get extensive experience of the day-to-day activity in a retail florist. I got to see what it was like on both quiet days and hectic days. I learned how to assist customers, how to listen closely to their requests and how to get further information when necessary by asking them appropriate questions. I used a cash register and the credit card and laser card machines every day that I was in the shop. I built up my self-confidence to a level where I know I can do a valuable day's work. I also improved my interpersonal skills that will be of benefit to me in any future work.

The discipline required to commit myself to attend full-time classes and to be on time for work experience has helped me to bridge the gap between working in the home and going out to work again. It is very beneficial being able to look forward to having a qualification that shows prospective employers that you have been independently assessed and have attained a certain standard.

On the negative side, I didn't get much of an opportunity to arrange flowers in foam nor did I learn everything about running a retail flower business. That was too much to expect in such a short time. I feel I need to gain considerable experience yet before I am confident enough to produce arrangements, wreaths, etc., for sale but I aim to get to this level of proficiency in the future.

Overall, at the end of my work experience I felt I'd become a useful member of staff and that my work experience has been a success. This has been confirmed by the fact that I've been asked if I'd be interested in working with Marie's Flowers when I finish my studies.

As regards further training, my next goal is to do the Interflora exams so that I'll have widely recognised qualifications. I also intend to set up my own business sometime in the future, after I gain even further floristry and interior landscaping experience.

Work Experience Diary

Work Experience Diary - Day 1

Name: _____   Work Experience Day(s): _____

Class: _____   Date(s): _____

Work Undertaken (List tasks): _____

_____

_____

Existing Skills Improved Upon:

1. Practical Skills   _____

2. Personal Skills   _____

3. Interpersonal Skills   _____

New Skills Learned:

1. Practical Skills   _____

2. Personal Skills   _____

3. Interpersonal Skills   _____

How Work Was Handled: _____

_____

_____

Challenges Encountered: _____

1. Personal Challenges   _____

2. Work-Related Challenges   _____

Other Comments: _____

_____

_____

Work Experience Diary - Day 2

Name: _____   Work Experience Day(s): _____

Class: _____   Date(s): _____

Work Undertaken (List tasks):   _____

_____

_____

Existing Skills Improved Upon:

1. Practical Skills   _____

2. Personal Skills   _____

3. Interpersonal Skills   _____

New Skills Learned:

1. Practical Skills   _____

2. Personal Skills   _____

3. Interpersonal Skills   _____

How Work Was Handled: _____

_____

_____

Challenges Encountered: _____

1. Personal Challenges   _____

2. Work-Related Challenges   _____

Other Comments: _____

_____

_____

Work Experience Diary - Day 3

Name: _____   Work Experience Day(s): _____

Class: _____   Date(s): _____

Work Undertaken (List tasks): _____

_____

_____

Existing Skills Improved Upon:

1. Practical Skills   _____

2. Personal Skills   _____

3. Interpersonal Skills   _____

New Skills Learned:

1. Practical Skills   _____

2. Personal Skills   _____

3. Interpersonal Skills   _____

How Work Was Handled: _____

_____

_____

Challenges Encountered: _____

1. Personal Challenges   _____

2. Work-Related Challenges   _____

Other Comments: _____

_____

_____

Work Experience Diary - Day 4

Name: _____   Work Experience Day(s): _____

Class: _____   Date(s): _____

Work Undertaken (List tasks):   _____

_____

_____

Existing Skills Improved Upon:

1. Practical Skills   _____

2. Personal Skills   _____

3. Interpersonal Skills   _____

New Skills Learned:

1. Practical Skills   _____

2. Personal Skills   _____

3. Interpersonal Skills   _____

How Work Was Handled: _____

_____

_____

Challenges Encountered: _____

1. Personal Challenges   _____

2. Work-Related Challenges   _____

Other Comments: _____

_____

_____

Work Experience Diary - Day 5

Name: _____   Work Experience Day(s): _____

Class: _____   Date(s): _____

Work Undertaken (List tasks): _____

_____

_____

Existing Skills Improved Upon:

1. Practical Skills   _____

2. Personal Skills   _____

3. Interpersonal Skills   _____

New Skills Learned:

1. Practical Skills   _____

2. Personal Skills   _____

3. Interpersonal Skills   _____

How Work Was Handled: _____

_____

_____

Challenges Encountered: _____

1. Personal Challenges   _____

2. Work-Related Challenges   _____

Other Comments: _____

_____

_____

Work Experience Diary - Day 6

Name: _____ Work Experience Day(s): _____

Class: _____ Date(s): _____

Work Undertaken (List tasks): _____

_____

_____

Existing Skills Improved Upon:

1. Practical Skills _____

2. Personal Skills _____

3. Interpersonal Skills _____

New Skills Learned:

1. Practical Skills _____

2. Personal Skills _____

3. Interpersonal Skills _____

How Work Was Handled: _____

_____

_____

Challenges Encountered: _____

1. Personal Challenges _____

2. Work-Related Challenges _____

Other Comments: _____

_____

_____

Work Experience Diary - Day 7

Name: _____   Work Experience Day(s): _____

Class: _____   Date(s): _____

Work Undertaken (List tasks): _____

_____

_____

Existing Skills Improved Upon:

1. Practical Skills   _____

2. Personal Skills   _____

3. Interpersonal Skills   _____

New Skills Learned:

1. Practical Skills   _____

2. Personal Skills   _____

3. Interpersonal Skills   _____

How Work Was Handled: _____

_____

_____

Challenges Encountered: _____

1. Personal Challenges   _____

2. Work-Related Challenges   _____

Other Comments: _____

_____

_____

Work Experience Diary - Day 8

Name: _____ Work Experience Day(s): _____

Class: _____ Date(s): _____

Work Undertaken (List tasks): _____

_____

_____

Existing Skills Improved Upon:

1. Practical Skills _____

2. Personal Skills _____

3. Interpersonal Skills _____

New Skills Learned:

1. Practical Skills _____

2. Personal Skills _____

3. Interpersonal Skills _____

How Work Was Handled: _____

_____

_____

Challenges Encountered: _____

1. Personal Challenges _____

2. Work-Related Challenges _____

Other Comments: _____

_____

_____

Work Experience Diary - Day 9

Name: _____   Work Experience Day(s): _____

Class: _____   Date(s): _____

Work Undertaken (List tasks): _____

_____

_____

Existing Skills Improved Upon:

1. Practical Skills   _____

2. Personal Skills   _____

3. Interpersonal Skills   _____

New Skills Learned:

1. Practical Skills   _____

2. Personal Skills   _____

3. Interpersonal Skills   _____

How Work Was Handled: _____

_____

_____

Challenges Encountered: _____

1. Personal Challenges   _____

2. Work-Related Challenges   _____

Other Comments: _____

_____

_____

Work Experience Diary - Day 10

Name: _____   Work Experience Day(s): _____

Class: _____   Date(s): _____

Work Undertaken (List tasks): _____

_____

_____

Existing Skills Improved Upon:

1. Practical Skills _____

2. Personal Skills _____

3. Interpersonal Skills _____

New Skills Learned:

1. Practical Skills _____

2. Personal Skills _____

3. Interpersonal Skills _____

How Work Was Handled: _____

_____

_____

Challenges Encountered: _____

1. Personal Challenges _____

2. Work-Related Challenges _____

Other Comments: _____

_____

_____

Work Experience Diary - Day 11

Name: _____   Work Experience Day(s): _____

Class: _____   Date(s): _____

Work Undertaken (List tasks): _____

_____

_____

Existing Skills Improved Upon:

1. Practical Skills   _____

2. Personal Skills   _____

3. Interpersonal Skills   _____

New Skills Learned:

1. Practical Skills   _____

2. Personal Skills   _____

3. Interpersonal Skills   _____

How Work Was Handled: _____

_____

_____

Challenges Encountered: _____

1. Personal Challenges   _____

2. Work-Related Challenges _____

Other Comments: _____

_____

_____

Work Experience Diary - Day 12

Name: _____   Work Experience Day(s): _____

Class: _____   Date(s): _____

Work Undertaken (List tasks):   _____

_____

_____

Existing Skills Improved Upon:

1. Practical Skills   _____

2. Personal Skills   _____

3. Interpersonal Skills   _____

New Skills Learned:

1. Practical Skills   _____

2. Personal Skills   _____

3. Interpersonal Skills   _____

How Work Was Handled: _____

_____

_____

Challenges Encountered: _____

1. Personal Challenges   _____

2. Work-Related Challenges   _____

Other Comments: _____

_____

_____

Work Experience Diary - Day 13

Name: _____   Work Experience Day(s): _____

Class: _____   Date(s): _____

Work Undertaken (List tasks): _____

_____

_____

Existing Skills Improved Upon:

1. Practical Skills   _____

2. Personal Skills   _____

3. Interpersonal Skills   _____

New Skills Learned:

1. Practical Skills   _____

2. Personal Skills   _____

3. Interpersonal Skills   _____

How Work Was Handled: _____

_____

_____

Challenges Encountered: _____

1. Personal Challenges   _____

2. Work-Related Challenges   _____

Other Comments: _____

_____

_____

Work Experience Diary - Day 14

Name: _____ Work Experience Day(s): _____

Class: _____ Date(s): _____

Work Undertaken (List tasks): _____

_____

_____

Existing Skills Improved Upon:

1. Practical Skills _____

2. Personal Skills _____

3. Interpersonal Skills _____

New Skills Learned:

1. Practical Skills _____

2. Personal Skills _____

3. Interpersonal Skills _____

How Work Was Handled: _____

_____

_____

Challenges Encountered: _____

1. Personal Challenges _____

2. Work-Related Challenges _____

Other Comments: _____

_____

_____

Work Experience Diary - Day 15

Name: _____ Work Experience Day(s): _____

Class: _____ Date(s): _____

Work Undertaken (List tasks): _____

_____

_____

Existing Skills Improved Upon:

1. Practical Skills _____

2. Personal Skills _____

3. Interpersonal Skills _____

New Skills Learned:

1. Practical Skills _____

2. Personal Skills _____

3. Interpersonal Skills _____

How Work Was Handled: _____

_____

_____

Challenges Encountered: _____

1. Personal Challenges _____

2. Work-Related Challenges _____

Other Comments: _____

_____

_____